EUREKA RESULTS

EUREKA RESULTS

HOW ENTREPRENEURS CAN TURN THEIR BEST IDEAS INTO REALITY

ASHLEE BERGHOFF

NEW DEGREE PRESS

EUREKA RESULTS

How Entrepreneurs Can Turn Their Best Ideas into Reality

ISBN 978-1-63676-726-0 *Paperback*
978-1-63730-041-1 *Kindle Ebook*
978-1-63730-143-2 *Ebook*

In memory of Pat Henriques, who insisted that I could make my best ideas happen.

In gratitude to the entrepreneurs in my family. By building something meaningful with your own two hands, you have made the world better. The Stafford and Campbell clans have constructed buildings, crafted furniture, sold hot dogs, raised cattle, smoked ribs, hawked bikes, advised leaders, rented homes, staged mansions, managed money, created culinary masterpieces, cultivated fitness, counseled people, and more. It means a lot to follow in your footsteps.

And to Pizza Hut, for using a pizza bribery system to turn me into a reader/English major/nerd/author.

TABLE OF CONTENTS

*"There are some people who live in a dream world,
and there are some who face reality; and then
there are those who turn one into the other."*

—DOUGLAS EVERETT

INTRODUCTION

You can tell what people love by how many different words they have for the same idea. Think, for example, about the sudden lightning bolt of a creative idea. It's a great feeling, isn't it? Turns out, we have a lot of great ways to describe it:

Eureka moment

Epiphany

Lightbulb moment

Flash of insight

Aha moment

Inspiration

Bombshell discovery

We love these moments, don't we? We want more of them. We measure our creativity by them. We judge our coaches and trainers by how many of these moments they give us. We expect these moments to launch us into success and be the hinge on our "hockey stick" of growth.

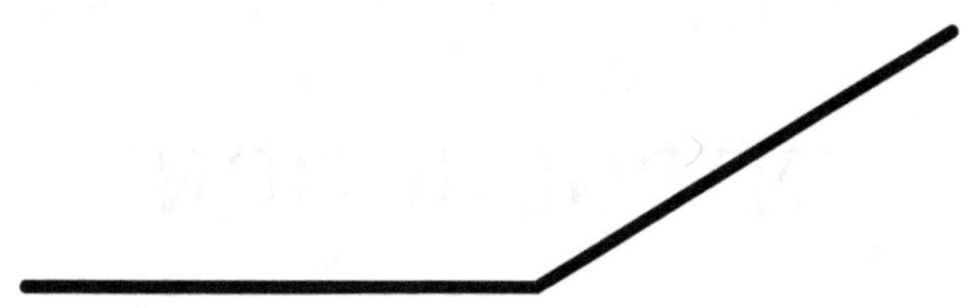

BUT HOW OFTEN DO OUR EUREKA MOMENTS ACTUALLY DO THAT FOR US?

I began my business with a mission to make order out of chaos for small business owners. I wanted to clear the clouds, remove obstacles, and give them breathing space in their businesses. And that's exactly what I did.

My clients came to me with whatever problems they had and I fixed them. They were happy; I felt fulfilled. I interacted with incredible entrepreneurs in the early stages of building a business they loved. The freedom to pursue a big dream was intoxicating.

But I began to notice something. I'd meet entrepreneurs who were discouraged and in the same place they were a year ago. They felt stuck. Their brains were crowded with a million projects and tasks and ideas, and they couldn't see clearly through it all.

Then, like a flash, a new insight or idea would break through. There it was—the shining solution; the moment they were waiting for! With the new idea came energy, forward motion, and hope. They'd strike off boldly to make their new idea happen.

The first few weeks would be amazing—ideas would flow, things would start to come together, and quick wins would fuel more progress. But after a few more weeks, the idea would lose its shine. It wasn't fun anymore. They'd hit a wall somewhere with a task they didn't want to do, a result that wasn't what they hoped, or a technical obstacle. They'd sink into the discouragement they felt before, convinced their lack of success was due to their own failure or the failure of their idea. So they would buy another course, listen to another webinar, or brainstorm on masterminds with their friends; a new idea would come, and another boost of hope and energy would come with it. But the cycle would continue year after year with no hockey stick growth curves in sight.

This cycle didn't just impact my friends' quality of life. According to the Bureau of Labor, only 50 percent of businesses survive past five years.[1] And even though all of us are listening to gurus painting a vision of millions, over 85 percent of us earn less than $100,000 a year in revenue.[2] Is it because our lightbulb moments aren't that great? Or is it because of something else? What's getting in our way?

---

1 Georgia McIntyre, "What Percentage of Small Businesses Fail? (and Other Need-to-Know Stats)," *Fundera* (blog), last modified November 20, 2020.

2 Nina Godlewski, "Small Business Revenue Statistics (2021): Annual Sales and Earnings," *Fundera*, last modified December 16, 2020.

I began to study the stories of the world's most high-income entrepreneurs—the men and women who built multimillion-dollar service businesses. I wanted to understand what made them different, what got them those rare, exponential results. Often, I noticed their short bio sounded something like this:

"I started out in my garage, and everything was tough. We were living on ramen noodles, and I made every mistake in the book. Then, one day in the shower it hit me—*this* was the thing I was meant to do instead. Eighteen months later, I hit seven figures, and now we're changing the world."

There it was, our expected eureka moment changing everything:

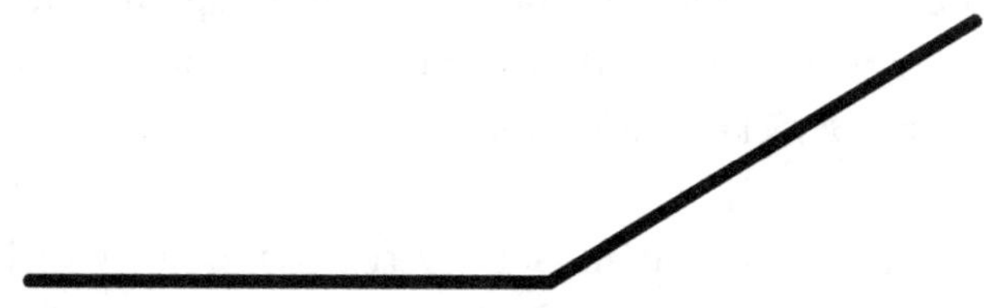

But then I dug deeper. These same entrepreneurs would share more of their story in their books and on podcasts, and I was able to map out a clearer picture. It looked a whole lot more like this:

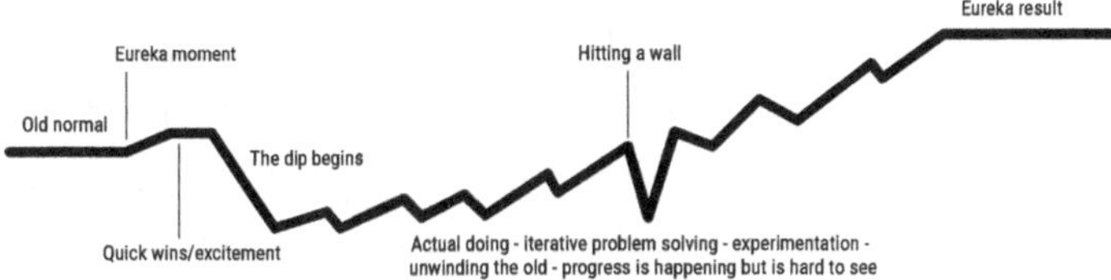

At first, I was frustrated. It felt like a bait and switch—like all the big players were lying to us about what it took for them to achieve their success. But after watching several of them for long enough, I knew that many of them wanted to help their fellow entrepreneurs succeed.

The actual reason for this simplistic story arc turns out to be much less sinister:

time + hindsight + the need to tell a quick story with a happy ending = a much smoother picture than what those entrepreneurs lived.

It reminds me of how I might tell you about my experience of learning to play the piano. I would start with the day at our family cabin when I plunked on the keys of our dilapidated upright and decided I wanted to play *Für Elise*. Then I would tell you about my amazing teacher and our annual Halloween recitals. I wouldn't bore you with a detailed account of the thirty minutes of daily practice spanning eight years of my childhood.

When successful entrepreneurs tell you about the moments that changed the game for them, they're not lying; those eureka moments *did* matter. Those are the moments that tend to stand out when we look back on them. But we need to see the bigger picture: there is a marathon between our eureka moment and its eureka *result* (the beautiful outcome we envision). We must be ready for the long haul. If we expect immediate, exponential results and find ourselves in the midst of practice and difficult labor instead, we will suffer unnecessarily.

We could listen to our heroes and decide these people are freaks of nature—inherently better than us—or we could recognize what's going on behind the scenes and get the tools we need for the roller-coaster ride of real entrepreneurship.

So, what are those tools?

DO WE NEED TO TOUGHEN UP?

Eureka moments are real and powerful. When we have them, we get a rush of excitement and a feeling of the road opening before our feet. But after the burst of energy and quick wins, the dip soon follows.

Running this marathon is hard. Things tend to take longer than we expected. We'll feel resistance from our brain telling us it was safer where we were before. We'll be tempted by new, shiny objects and beckoned by distractions. We'll acutely feel our waning creative energy and start wishing for more. We'll be making progress, but we won't see it.

How do we get through this in one piece?

Maybe the answer is another set of words we have available to us:

Grit

Resilience

Endurance

Perseverance

Tenacity

Is gritting your teeth and pushing through enough? Is the answer just more willpower?

I've met too many entrepreneurs for this to make sense either. We all have bruised shoulders from throwing our weight against a few boulders we were trying to move. We've all told ourselves to keep going when things get tough. We've endured pain and failure before, and we're all pretty determined to never go back to our old corporate lives. Entrepreneurs who feel stuck can be every bit as tenacious as the ones in the top 1 percent of their markets.

So, the problem can't be that we're not resilient enough either. "Toughing it out" isn't doing the trick for us. We may have made it this far by pure force of will, but we can't build a career that way (at least, if we want to avoid ulcers and heart attacks).

INSPIRATION + GRIT + ?

Eureka moments are fantastic. Endurance is important too.

They're just not enough on their own.

After months of research and studying the stories of hundreds of entrepreneurs, I'm convinced that relying on a combination of creative insights and toughness is like loading up on carbs the night before a marathon, getting all pumped up with our favorite songs, and then running the race barefoot and without a water bottle.

What's the entrepreneurship equivalent of shoes and a backpack filled with supplies? How are people going the distance?

As I asked business owners this question, their answers varied. They shared stories about community, mentorship, and the right team members. Mindset shifts, planning, taking focused action, and refining their business model mattered too. I peeled back the layers to see if there was a single theme to these things, a connecting element that every entrepreneur needs.

When I found it, it was like lifting a rug and popping up a wood board to find a solid concrete foundation hidden underneath—nothing amazing to look at, but steady enough to build a business on.

What I found was that every single tool an entrepreneur mentioned was undergirded by a system.

Every strategy, relationship, and amazing outcome was enabled, strengthened, and maintained by some kind of structure—often invisible, sometimes unintentional, but there all the same.

It was like in nature, where trees grow from a strong network of roots that dig through soil into a water source and squirrels bury nuts every fall to survive the winter.

Or like shoes and a backpack, both of which are systems in and of themselves. We live in a world filled with many different pieces, all brought together through order and structure.

For entrepreneurs, these systems showed up as routines, frameworks, and habits. People would find what worked and stick with it, or act out an insight they learned, or cultivate what mattered to them. The more intentional their systems were, the stronger the foundation became. Entrepreneurs who knew how to leverage their systems could create businesses with staying power—businesses that could stand strong for years, even decades. The insights and strategies they gathered along the way would work for them. The changes they made stuck and the plans they made happened.

YOUR NEW SECRET WEAPON

When you add systems to your best ideas and the determination you already bring to your work every day, something amazing happens—those ideas stop being ideas. They become part of your reality instead.

I know this isn't the answer most entrepreneurs want to hear. All this buildup to *the* answer, the *one* thing that can make inspiration and grit turn into reality, and the pot at the end of the rainbow is...systems?

If you find systems frustrating, you're not alone. We tend to believe they stifle all creative energy. They're the wet blanket on top of all our lightbulb moments, the death of serendipity. Aren't systems the cause of bureaucracy and the phrase "but we've always done it this way?"

But that's the point, isn't it? Systems are the powerful structures determining what *actually* happens rather than what we want to happen or what we say should happen. When systems are bad, they make progress difficult. When systems are good, they make progress inevitable.

Systems turn ideas into reality. Without them, ideas don't become reality. Without them, *your* ideas won't become reality.

But systems don't simply work—when you see them for what they are, they can become beautiful. Think of nature's most beautiful systems—things like honeycombs, snowflakes, or weeping willows—but imagine them inside your business instead of outside your door. The right systems can be an elegant expression of who you are and what you want your life to be.

YOUR POWER TO WIELD GREAT SYSTEMS

I'm on a mission to help you see the beauty and power of systems, but even more than that, to harness that power in your life. This book is meant to give you the framework and structure you need to build the business you imagine and protect what matters most to you.

First, I'll redefine what systems are and how thinking about them differently will revolutionize your business (and, frankly, your life).

I'll move on to talk about how your mindset is the foundation for the right systems and what principles you can leverage to build resilience through the journey from insight to result.

Finally, I'll talk specifically about five key areas in which you can use systems to transform your business: your vision, time management, operational structure, metrics, and team.

Along the way, I'll share real stories from entrepreneurs so you can see this happen in real life.

Systems don't have to be the straitjacket in your business. Instead, they can be the tools giving you hope, momentum, and energy throughout the journey. The right systems will break your addiction to the hit of eureka moments and keep you from making the marathon of life harder than it has to be.

This field guide is your backpack full of water and granola bars and a note from your mom saying you're doing a great job.

Don't leave home without it.

WHY LISTEN TO ME?

I have loved systems ever since I created report cards for my stuffed animals at the age of eight. I've built them, used them, fixed them, and benefited from them in every job I've ever had, from a restaurant to small local businesses to an international anti-trafficking organization to a publicly-traded consulting firm. I also studied systems while earning my MBA at Georgetown University. In 2017, I was ready to strike out on my own and build a vocation around the lifestyle I wanted for my family, so I started my own business—A Squared Online. Since then, I have helped dozens of entrepreneurs leverage the power of systems in their businesses. Systems are my passion, and I wrote this book to share that passion with you.

WHO IS THIS BOOK FOR?

No matter who you are, systems can be a powerful tool for you. I focused my stories and examples on entrepreneurs in general, and lifestyle-driven entrepreneurs in particular, for two reasons:

- I am an entrepreneur, and I work with entrepreneurs every day. Many of my stories will be the most relevant for that group of people.
- If you started a business for freedom and to cultivate a certain lifestyle (whether that be flexibility around building a family, living as a digital nomad, pursuing a variety of passions, providing space for rest as you live with a chronic illness, or any of a dozen more reasons), you might find yourself trapped in a world where you work

harder than you've ever worked before, and you feel less free. I hate this, and I want to change it.

If you're running a start-up that you intend to grow rapidly and sell rather than a lifestyle business you want to maintain long-term, this book will still be valuable. Systems are critical to scaling any business effectively. The stories may sound different, but the concepts are the same for any type of business.

Systems show up everywhere, so understanding how they work can be helpful for a career within a company, building a home, developing your skills, or even raising children. I hope more and more people start to see systems as a valuable tool instead of a chore, so no matter who you are, the ideas here will be relevant to you. As you read, think about how these concepts can apply to your situation. For example, as you read about metrics, think about tracking what matters to you in achieving a weight loss goal or adding more celebration into your home life. As you learn about the difference between complicated and complex systems, think about how you can use those systems to strengthen your marriage or help your child navigate a tough school subject.

Now that we know what we're up to, let's start by defining exactly what systems are and how they work. I hope you enjoy this journey!

harder than you've ever worked before, and you feel less free. I hate that, and I want to change it.

If you're running a small business and want to grow rapidly and sell rather than a lifestyle business you want to maintain long-term, this book will still be valuable. Systems are critical to scaling any business, and while the terminology may sound different, the concepts are the same for any type of business.

Systems are everywhere, and understanding how they work can help in all areas of life: running a company, building a home, developing your skills, or even raising children. [illegible] more and more perceptive that [illegible] systems [illegible] of a chess [illegible] who [illegible] here [illegible] to you. As you read, think about how these concepts [illegible] apply to your situation [illegible] [illegible] [illegible] [illegible] complicated and complex systems. Think about how [illegible] help your child [illegible] through [illegible].

Now that we know what [illegible] defining exactly what a system [illegible] you enjoy this journey!

PART ONE

INSPIRATION + GRIT + ?

CHAPTER 1

SYSTEMS

Every system is perfectly designed
to get the results it gets.

—PAUL BATALDEN

Systems decide what happens in the world.

Somehow, though, we don't seem to have a great societal understanding of what systems are and why they have so much power.

The word "system" often conjures images of bureaucracy, software tools, mind-numbing charts, or process and procedure manuals. However, if we think about how we use the word, then we can see something deeper:

- School systems
- Support systems
- Belief systems
- The capitalist system

- Computer systems
- Digestive systems
- Root systems
- Justice systems
- The decimal system
- Ecosystems
- "All systems go"
- "Bucking the system"
- "Getting it out of his system"

There's a lot more here than a checklist or an overused corporate term. So what exactly is a system?

According to the *Oxford English Dictionary,* there are two official definitions for "system":

1. "A set of principles or procedures according to which something is done; an organized scheme or method" (a.k.a. "how something is done").
2. "A set of things working together as parts of a mechanism or an interconnecting network; a complex whole" (a.k.a. "individual elements working together as a unit").[3]

BOTTOM LINE: A SYSTEM IS HOW WE DO THINGS. IT'S HOW WE ORGANIZE PEOPLE, RESOURCES, AND IDEAS TOGETHER TO MAKE SENSE OF THINGS AND MAKE SOMETHING HAPPEN.

Systems are fascinating because we can deliberately design them, or they can be invisible to us. Whether we're aware of

3 *Lexico.com,* s.v. "system (n.)," accessed February 12, 2021.

them or not, our systems have a purpose and an outcome, and they achieve that outcome consistently.

At the moment, you may feel like you don't have many systems in your life or business. If you're a "fly by the seat of your pants" sort of person, the idea of organizing the elements of your life might sound less inspiring than allowing life to unfold organically. If this is you, one of the principles supporting how you live your life is spontaneity. You are, consciously or not, organizing your thoughts and behaviors around that idea. Your life system is designed for serendipity and the free flow of ideas. If you are happy with how things are going, then you have successfully used an unconscious system to get where you want to go! But if you aren't, it won't be enough to buy a new planner. You'll want to dig in and make some adjustments to that ingrained (dare I say, "systemic") way of thinking.

We can see the same trends happening at a much more macro level. For years, our country has been reckoning with what has been coined *systemic* racism. The argument is simple—even if our institutions are filled with good people who have no intention to act in racist ways, we can look at the data, see outcomes that are inequitable, and understand that something in the system should be addressed.[4] We may forever debate *why* the system is not working, *where* things have gone wrong, or *how* to fix it, but recognizing that a system exists can be a great starting point for a constructive conversation. Once a system has matured to encompass many people and

---

4 "Systemic Racism & Health Care, COVID & Treatment," National Institute for Health Care Management Foundation, accessed February 12, 2021.

deeply rooted cultures, processes, and principles, it can be filled to the brim with people who want the outcome to be different and *still get the outcome the system is structured to get.*

Systems are powerful.

Once you start thinking in terms of systems, you'll see them everywhere. But we don't like thinking about systems, which just so happens to be due to a belief system—individualism. Many of us as modern people believe in individual rights, individual freedoms, and individual reason.[5] We buck against the idea that we are influenced by systems, participate in systems in a way we didn't consciously choose, or cannot simply change our outcomes by changing our individual free choices in the moment. But here's the truth: we utilize and participate in dozens of systems every day. Some of them we choose, and some of them we don't. We do not have the power to change every system we encounter. However, we do have more power than we think, and recognizing when a system is at work is a critical first step.

"The myth of the self-made man... ignores the inescapable reality that no human is ever self-made, neither in the fabric of our being nor in our actions and judgments concerning the world. Unaware of our interdependence, ignorant of the countless

5 *New Dictionary of the History of Ideas*, s.v. "individualism," by Cary Nederman, accessed February 12, 2021.

ways that cultural dogmas influence our self-construction, we presume we are atomically alone in the choices we make."

—JOHN F. KAVANAUGH

When separate systems work together to make a cohesive whole, the impact is exponentially greater than any of those elements would have individually. You can find systems at work behind the rise and fall of nations, genocides, the curing of diseases, the development of our character, and the quality of our lives.[6] When we learn how to study the systems within and around us, we can harness that power for good.

"I WAS JUST DOING MY JOB."

I remember the moment clearly. After walking through the entire Holocaust Museum in Washington, DC, from top to bottom, I thought I was prepared for everything I'd see. But I had no idea there would be videos.

At the bottom of the museum, screens played preserved footage from the liberation of the concentration camps. Although I was horrified by the footage, what I remember most is watching soldiers leading German staff members out of various buildings. They all looked profoundly normal—secretaries, guards, cooks. If I saw them all behind me in the Target line, I wouldn't think anything of it.

6 Edward J. Watts, "The Fall of Rome and the Lessons for America," *Time*, December 15, 2018; "Armenian Genocide," *History.com*, October 31, 2019; Linton Weeks, "Defeating Polio, the Disease That Paralyzed America," *NPR History Dept.*, April 10, 2015; David Brooks, *The Road to Character* (New York: Random House Trade Paperbacks, 2016).

They were like me.

I, like many of us, had focused much of my energy on Hitler as the sole cause of the Holocaust. He was an evil individual with cruel intentions and great power. However, if Hitler had worked alone, he would have accomplished little and we would not be talking about him today. Instead, he knew how to leverage the economic, political, and philosophical systems in Germany at the time. He was able to motivate millions to join him. Many things helped Hitler gain and maintain power for years, including a difficult financial depression following WWI reparations, "the emotional vulnerability of an entire society," manufacturing and transportation systems, the global popularity of eugenics, and long-running suspicion of the Jewish community.[7]

While it might be more comfortable to imagine your average Nazi sympathizer in the 1930s as an abnormally immoral person, seeing the whole context can be more useful. We are responsible for our actions and we can learn from the past, striving to be better people in a healthier society, but we should also examine the systems that have contributed to history's greatest atrocities. Until we do, we will remain blissfully unaware of our own detrimental systems and the people hurt by them, comforting ourselves that we're inherently

---

7 Jennifer Llewellyn, Jim Southey, and Steve Thompson, "The Nazi Economic Recovery," *Alpha History*, July 16, 2020; Lucy Hughes-Hallett, "Fear, Shame, Guilt, Suicide: Ordinary Germans at the End of the Second World War," *NewStatesman*, August 21, 2019; David Grossman, "Study Shows Precisely How Nazi Infrastructure Enabled the Worst of the Holocaust," *Popular Mechanics*, January 2, 2019; "Eugenics," *History.com*, October 28, 2019; "Signs of German Antisemitism Before Hitler," *The Guardian*, September 9, 2009.

better people who would "never do" whatever we read about in the history books.

> *"We can't impose our will on a system. We can listen to what the system tells us and discover how its properties and our values can work together to bring forth something much better than could ever be produced by our will alone."*
>
> —DONELLA H. MEADOWS

When we don't take our systems seriously, the results can be devastating.

BACK TO BUSINESS

If you're reading this as an entrepreneur or a business owner, you might be wondering why we're talking about history and society in a book about business systems. But if you can see systems in these sweeping areas of human life, it's easier to recognize their impact in your own day-to-day business life.

Whatever outcomes you're experiencing in your business can be directly traced back to the systems supporting them.

When you can look objectively at what's happening in your business—especially the things you want to change—and can follow the thread back from that outcome to what allowed it to happen, you're in a great position to change the system and thus change the result.

IGNORE YOUR SYSTEMS AT YOUR OWN PERIL

If you're currently thinking, "That's nice, Ashlee, but I've gotten this far without paying any attention to my systems," you make a good point. Animals live their lives without any conscious attention to the systems that determine their lives (also known as instincts). You too have natural gifts, instincts, resilience, and some strokes of good luck that helped you make it this far. For example, your body has systems working without your conscious knowledge to keep you alive every single day. When your life systems are working, they will become completely invisible to you.

But what about when your systems are *not* working, or when you have outcomes in your life you don't want? That's when you'll want the tools in this book and the ability to pull that system out from hiding, slap it down in front of you on the table, and change what needs to change so you can get where you want to go.

WHEN SYSTEMS ARE NO LONGER OPTIONAL

Vicki Moore made revolutionary changes to her own systems after an unexpected crucible moment.

Vicki began her e-learning business as an independent consultant in 2002. After years of working for herself, she began to win larger and larger projects, nudging her to hire her first team members. A few years later, her sales suddenly accelerated, tripling the company's revenue in less than six months.

"I hadn't properly prepared for that rocket of growth," Vicki said. "I was the lead salesperson, managed the whole team, handled all our sales and marketing, and did a lot of the client and project management."

Vicki began to delegate as much as she could, but struggled to get support for more strategic responsibilities in the company. She was working over eighty hours each week and telling herself: "You're growing a business, and that means working long hours. This is what it takes." For years, she felt too busy to create a process, and it was easier for her to tackle something herself rather than hand it off to someone else.

One day while sitting at her computer, Vicki realized she couldn't see her screen. The light in the room was blinding, so she turned off all the lights and called her doctor. She then learned she wasn't experiencing a traumatic brain injury or traditional illness. Instead, Vicki was diagnosed with a rare eye disease that usually afflicts boxers and football players (people who regularly take direct hits to the face). "Overnight, I went from eighty hours a week to not being able to read my own emails," Vicki told me.

Thankfully, Vicki had an assistant she trusted. For the next two months, Vicki sat next to her assistant in the office and dictated her processes. "When the client says this, you should answer the question this way," she would say. From sales and marketing to operations and client management, Vicki defined everything. She learned to articulate, step by step, every aspect of her work until her business was so systemized, Vicki was able to accomplish in twenty hours what used to take eighty. The company's revenue continued to grow.

"Even knowing that (building processes) was the right thing to do, I didn't do it until I had to," Vicki said. "But it changed my life. I wasn't doing a four-hour workweek, but it was pretty dang close."

If you're too busy to create systems, you're not alone. Thinking about your systems when you're trying to keep your head above water isn't easy. But my hope for you is that you don't wait until something goes wrong to build intentional systems. You never know when they could change everything for you.

***

As a business owner, you have an incredible tool available to you—a powerful resource that you can't afford to ignore. When you notice your systems and design them with intention, they can revolutionize every aspect of your life. I hope you carry this new understanding into how you market, plan, serve your customers, pursue your dreams, and show up for the people you love, because it matters. Your systems can change your life.

In the coming chapters, I'll talk about how different systems work and then transition into the practical work of learning how to use them effectively.

KEY TAKEAWAYS FROM CHAPTER 1:

- A system is how we do things. It's how we organize people, resources, and ideas together to make something happen.

- Systems are powerful enough to override desires. We can want something to be different, but outcomes are determined by our systems.
- Systems still exist even if they're unconscious or invisible to you.
- The outcomes in your life and business can be traced back to the systems that support them.

CONTINUE READING TO LEARN ABOUT THE DIFFERENT TYPES OF SYSTEMS IN YOUR LIFE.

QUESTIONS FOR REFLECTION AND DISCUSSION:

1. What is an outcome in your life that you don't currently like? What systems are supporting that negative outcome?
2. Where are the areas of your life where you have been resisting systems or wanting to protect your creative freedom? Does a new understanding of systems relieve some of that tension and open up ways for your systems to strengthen your creative freedom?
3. What is one system you'd like to adjust within your life or business?

CHAPTER 2

TYPES OF SYSTEMS

"Systems and processes will always surpass motivation."

—CHRIS MATAKAS

Systems are how we do things. They're the interconnected structures that determine what happens.

Not all systems are created equal. When you own a business, you'll find yourself navigating a whole sea of systems every day. It's impossible to *live* without them, much less work. When you train yourself to see and use those systems intentionally, you'll tap into some of the most powerful structures in your life.

As I type this paragraph right now, I'm benefiting from a variety of different systems. Systems in my body are keeping me breathing and upright. The inner workings of my keyboard and computer enable me to skip a pen and paper. Training enabled me to use the English language, to read, and to write.

Planning helped me set aside this time on a Friday morning to write while my husband and daughter eat breakfast downstairs. Structures, outlines, and accountability mechanisms helped me write this book.

How can we begin to tease apart the differences between these types of systems and how we can use them?

In their *Harvard Business Review* article, David Snowden and Mary Boone introduce the four main types of systems discussed in systems theory:

- Simple
- Complicated
- Complex
- Chaotic[8]

Right now, you are currently surrounded by dozens of each of these, and each one plays an important role in your business.

SIMPLE SYSTEMS INVOLVE ONE PATH TO ONE ANSWER

This morning, I brushed my teeth. I have one toothbrush, one tube of toothpaste, and one set of teeth. Every time I brush my teeth, I do the exact same thing. Sure, I might get a little rebellious and buy a different brand of toothpaste sometimes, but most of the time, my brain is elsewhere entirely while I'm following this *simple system*.

---

8 David J. Snowden and Mary E. Boone, "A Leader's Framework for Decision Making," *Harvard Business Review*, November 2007.

Other simple systems include:

- Onboarding your clients
- Tracking your metrics
- Answering emails
- Posting predefined content to social media
- Bookkeeping
- Setting up software tools
- Updating plug-ins on your website
- Daily planning and other daily habits or practices

When you following a simple system, you know exactly what the result should be and follow a chain of cause and effect all the way through the process. When something breaks, all you have to do is "identify the problem...categorize it...and respond appropriately."[9]

COMPLICATED SYSTEMS HAVE MULTIPLE POTENTIAL RIGHT ANSWERS AND MANY MORE MOVING PARTS

A few days ago, my computer monitors shut off without warning. Thankfully, I'm married to a software engineer. He pulled out the computer tower, unscrewed some things while experimenting with various solutions, and declared we had a problem with the graphics card. The solution? Turning the computer off and back on again.

Computers, cars, and other high-end machines are great examples of complicated systems. When you work in a

9 Brad Feld, "Simple, Complicated, and Complex Systems," *Feld Thoughts* (blog), March 28, 2019.

complicated system, you'll find a number of different moving parts. Often, multiple simple systems work together to make a more complicated system work. You can still have a single thread of cause and effect flowing through a complicated system, but it might take more expertise to see.

In your business, complicated systems include:

- Your customer experience process
- Your sales process
- Solving a consulting problem for a client
- Your team working together on a specific project
- Your marketing plan
- Financial management
- Project management
- Your time management habits
- Your ten-year plan

To adjust a broken complicated system, it's not enough to categorize the problem. You will also need to analyze your options and choose between multiple potential solutions.[10]

COMPLEX SYSTEMS ARE DYNAMIC AND DON'T HAVE CLEAR "RIGHT" OR "WRONG" ANSWERS. THE OUTCOMES OF A COMPLEX SYSTEM CAN BE MIXED, TOO, WITH BOTH POSITIVE AND NEGATIVE IMPACTS STREAMING FROM THE SAME PLACE

You'll know you're dealing with a complex system when mapping out a process of cause and effect to a straightforward answer is impossible. You can't exactly find a "right"

---

10 Snowden and Boone, "A Leader's Framework for Decision Making."

answer for Chicago, for instance. You can make choices that strengthen a city or improve the lives of many people living in it, but no city is perfect.

Another sign of a complex system is that it transcends the sum of its parts. You can learn how a car (a complicated system) works by examining its component parts and seeing how they fit together. If you tried to do the same with a person, though, you wouldn't even come close to capturing the essence of who they are.

Your business is a great example of a complex system. You can't turn it into a checklist, there are many potential right answers, and the relationship between your ideas and reality is constantly evolving. As an entrepreneur, I live in a complex system. As I grow and change, I often feel like the ground shifts under my feet right after I've figured it all out. What worked when I was a first-year founder doesn't work anymore. Although I can give everything I have to being the best entrepreneur possible, I will inevitably fail sometimes. Aspects of my work will do inadvertent damage, just as others will have a positive impact far beyond my expectations. I have to be openhanded about my entrepreneurial journey, but I can still leverage simple systems (like daily mindset work and clear planning) to add helpful structure to my work and the platform for a strong business.

Other examples of complex systems include:

- Marriage
- Culture
- Parenting

- Cities
- The economy
- Our global ecosystem
- Governments
- Your physical health
- Your values and beliefs
- Your mindset and mental health
- Your business's vision and reason for existing
- Your team
- Your life

Unlike complicated or simple systems, complex systems don't always "break" in an immediate and obvious way. Instead, problems can wear down the system over time. Because of this, solving a problem in a complex system isn't about categorizing the problem or analyzing optional solutions, but about visualizing the dynamics between the connected elements and looking for patterns.[11]

Complex systems are where the rubber meets the road. The impact of complex systems extends far beyond what we might expect by looking at the simple systems that make them up. That's why understanding and harnessing them matters so much.

CHAOTIC SYSTEMS

Sometimes, chaos occurs. If you were running a restaurant in March of 2020, the lockdown of your entire industry due to COVID-19 was unprecedented and destructive. When

11 Ibid.

emergencies or sudden violent changes upend everything, your world can change in an instant. At that point, your goal as a leader is "not to discover patterns but to stanch the bleeding."[12] If you can take action to find some stability and room to think, you can revert into the realm of complexity and move forward. In 2020, many restaurant owners applied for emergency funds and minimized their teams before building up a takeout business or finding other creative solutions.

We won't study chaotic systems in this book, but knowing they exist can help you recognize when it's time to triage and move out of "emergency mode" as quickly as possible. If you are putting out fires on a regular basis, then you could be living in a chaotic system of your own design. You can use the principles in this book to step out of chaos and into complexity.

SYSTEMS WORKING TOGETHER

Simple, complicated, and complex systems work together to give shape to your daily life. Most of the time, you're using a combination of all three to pursue your goals and build your business.

Imagine you're working with a client to solve a problem with their profitability. Without even noticing it, you're using multiple systems:

- Locating their past revenue data (simple)
- Evaluating their pricing (complicated)

---

12 Ibid.

- Considering problems in their team culture that impact retention (complex)
- Discussing their vision for their business (complex)
- Defining a new process for lead generation (complicated)
- Invoicing the client at the end of the project (simple)

Each of these systems can be seen and improved as independent units, but always with an understanding that each system has a much broader impact. Even talking about your client's revenue data can lead you straight into the big questions about their sense of worth, their vision for their future, or the reason they started their business in the first place.

As you study your systems, you can also trace your simple and complicated systems to a complex system they exist to support. Complex systems are the deepest elements of our lives and all other systems flow into them eventually.

Here are some examples:

- Atoms (simple) → the circulatory system (complicated) → a healthy body (complex)
- Onboarding your clients → a strong customer experience → a healthy business
- Tracking the size of your email list → clear marketing metrics → an effective marketing strategy
- Buying a cake → team celebrations → a strong company culture
- A daily planning routine → effective time management → living in alignment with your priorities

When you can visualize the systems in your life and how they work together, you'll be able to trace those impacts and make wiser decisions.

***

The systems of our lives are important, varied, and interconnected. That's all great to know. But where do we go from here? How do we *use* these systems? In the next three chapters, we'll dig into how you can use simple, complicated, and complex systems to strengthen your business.

KEY TAKEAWAYS FROM CHAPTER 2:

- Systems can be classified as simple, complicated, and complex.
- Simple systems involve a single path to a single right answer.
- Complicated systems have multiple potential right answers and many more moving parts.
- Complex systems are dynamic, fundamental, and vital—they decide the tenor of our lives and can alter the course of history. Simple and complicated systems flow into complex systems and contribute to their strengths or weaknesses.

CONTINUE READING TO LEARN HOW SIMPLE SYSTEMS WORK AND HOW YOU CAN USE THEM.

QUESTIONS FOR REFLECTION AND DISCUSSION:

1. Look around you. Pick out five systems in your immediate vicinity and classify them—are they simple, complicated, or complex?
2. What are the most valuable complex systems in your own life?
3. If someone watched you go about your day, would they be able to identify which complex systems are most important to you? If not, where can you adapt your daily habits to align to your values?

CHAPTER 3

HOW SIMPLE SYSTEMS WORK

"Systems equal profit...and they make everyone more happy and less crazy."

—RACHEL RODGERS

Simple systems may be the easiest for us to get our minds around, but they can also be the most difficult to deal with. Many simple systems are the opposite of easy or automatic. There may be a clear path to a single answer, but determining the right path or innovating a new answer can take years of study and skill.

The lightbulb, for instance, is a simple system. Most of us would struggle to make a lightbulb ourselves, and its invention was a world-changing discovery. Calling it "simple" doesn't make it any less of a powerful tool—it simply means that when an LED lightbulb gets made, there is one clear path to one clear answer. Any deviation from that path will probably turn into every company's nightmare—a recall.

In your business, some simple systems might feel like a big pile of minutiae you have to deal with all the time. This is where posting your blog on your website lands, or chasing down an unpaid invoice, or answering an email. One of the potential traps of simple systems is that you might be tempted to think about them as little as possible. You just do them and then move on to things that feel more important.

But when you don't make conscious decisions about what belongs in your simple systems, they will pile up and drain your time and energy.

Steven Covey—a productivity expert and author of *The Seven Habits of Highly Effective People*—was famous for introducing the world to the concept of "big rocks."[13] The concept stuck so well because it was so visual. In one of his classic talks, Covey brought up a member of the audience and then filled a bucket three-fourths full of bright green pebbles, explaining that they represented "all these little, small things that tend to fill our lives." Then, he pointed to multiple larger rocks on the table, each labeled with important things like "family time," "quarterly planning," or "new product development," and instructed the audience member to add them to the bucket without stacking them above the top rim. As the woman dug into the gravel to make space for each rock, Covey talked about the tradeoffs as it became clear she would be unable to add them all. As the "vacation" rock left the bucket to make

---

13 Stephen R. Covey, "Big Rocks," *Franklin Covey,* video, 04:01.

space for an "urgent and important" rock, Covey asked the audience if any of this felt familiar. Murmurs of agreement filled the room.

Another empty bucket sat next to the full one and Covey nodded toward it. "You can take a whole different approach... you have a fresh bowl," he suggested. The woman looked at it and said she wanted to put in the big rocks first. Together, they read out the name of each big rock as it settled into the bucket. Then, the woman dumped the pebbles over the big rocks, filling it to the top without overflowing it. She beamed with pride as the audience applauded.[14]

Covey had found a brilliant way to demonstrate that if we start with the big rocks—the bigger projects that mean the most to us—we can often fit quite a few of the smaller tasks into the gaps left behind. But if we start with the smaller stuff, it tends to take up all the space, making it impossible to fit the big rocks in later.[15]

What's interesting, though, is that even the big rocks are a combination of smaller ones. "Quarterly planning" is likely to involve gathering data, setting up a team meeting, or doing research. "Vacation" requires hundreds of small tasks to be completed, from buying travel-sized sunscreen to finding a pet sitter to picking a hotel at your destination. The question isn't *whether* we're completing simple tasks and projects, but what they're meant to do and how well they align with our biggest, most important priorities.

---

14 Ibid.

15 Ibid.

So how do we do this? How do we use simple systems to build toward the big, important things rather than letting an endless stream of tasks bury us?

When you're dealing with simple systems, there are three principles you can keep in mind: using simple systems to support complex ones, defining your simple systems, and troubleshooting bigger problems at the simple system level.

USE SIMPLE SYSTEMS TO SUPPORT THE COMPLEX SYSTEMS THAT MATTER TO YOU

As a human race, we tend to believe that complex systems are "purer" if we don't leverage simple systems to strengthen them. Love should just flow naturally. We should just remember everything about our friends. Inspiration should drive what we create, and when.

So much of what is beautiful in life comes in the unplanned moments, the sparks of inspiration that happen when we're not looking for them, and the hours we spend living instead of doing. It's true: the world would be worse off if all our most important moments turned into regimented systems and checklists. If we lived in alignment with our deepest values, we wouldn't need to spend a lot of time designing our systems. We could let the systems that happen naturally lead us to a rich life full of those moments.

But how many couples find themselves at the end of their marriage and realize they stopped making time for each other years ago?

How many parents look back on their kids' childhood and wish they'd spent less time running to keep up with a million activities and more time being together?

How many people on their deathbed regret the things they always dreamed of doing but never did?

We're human. We have a real tendency to miss what matters most to us without even realizing it. We bow to the tyranny of the urgent and let less important things crowd out the moments that add richness to our lives. As entrepreneurs, we're even more susceptible to this. We can spend years without ever "clocking out." We can hustle our way to external success without realizing the personal sacrifices we're making along the way.

We need conscious simple systems to protect what matters most to us. They sometimes feel a little too easy, but their impact can be revolutionary. Couples can schedule regular date nights or annual weekends away without the kids. Parents can set aside one day each week to hang out as a family without any activities. You can commit to spending thirty minutes every day taking a step toward your big dream.

Using your simple systems with intention will help you prioritize the big rocks rather than trying (in vain) to keep up with an endless deluge of urgent things that don't matter.

Many successful entrepreneurs and creators use intentional, simple systems daily:

- Oprah Winfrey meditates for twenty minutes twice a day[16]
- Kenneth Chenault spends time every evening planning for the next day[17]
- Brené Brown puts on her workout clothes as soon as she wakes up[18]
- Tim Ferris designed a five-step morning routine that he follows daily[19]
- Brad Feld and his wife have monthly "life dinners" to reflect on the past month, prepare for the one to come, and share a small gift with one another[20]
- Rachel Rodgers gets dressed for work every day, even though she works from home[21]
- Jack Dorsey has a theme for each day to cut down on multitasking[22]
- Evan Williams exercises in the middle of the day when his creative energy is lowest[23]

---

16 Oprah Winfrey, "What Oprah Knows for Sure about Finding the Fullest Expression of Yourself," *O, The Oprah Magazine*, February 2012.

17 Kaivan Dave, "Daily Morning Routine Habits of Successful CEOs," *Awesome Coffee*, October 7, 2020.

18 Annabel Nugent, "Tried and Tested: 3 Daily Routines of Mega-Successful Women," *XCityPlus*, March 2020.

19 "Inside Tim Ferriss' Morning Routine: The 5-Step Process to Win the Day," *BrainFlow*, accessed February 12, 2021.

20 Brad Feld, "Life Dinner," *Feld Thoughts* (blog), March 7, 2008.

21 "The Truth about Working from Home: 7 Keys for a More Beautiful + Productive Workspace," *The Chalkboard*, accessed February 12, 2021.

22 Kevin Kruse, "The Jack Dorsey Productivity Secret That Enables Him to Run Two Companies at Once," *Forbes*, October 12, 2015.

23 "Daily Routines and Habits of Highly Productive People," *Clockify*, accessed February 12, 2021.

- Daymond John has business and life goals that he reads both before he goes to bed and when he wakes up[24]

These simple systems (also known as routines) don't sap the meaning out of life. Instead, they become the structure that protects meaning, sets us up for success, and brings us back repeatedly to what matters most.

"The trick, I think, is to learn to appreciate each thing you do achieve—no matter how small or seemingly insignificant—as an integral part of the greater whole. This sentence completes the paragraph. That's a moment to recognise and savour. The paragraph, now completed, allows the book to become what I envisioned it would be, in tandem with all the other sentences and paragraphs over which I can take the same small pleasure."[25]

—LAURA GALE

DEFINE SIMPLE SYSTEMS CLEARLY AND MAKE DECISIONS ONCE WHENEVER POSSIBLE

Some systems, like regular protected time with your family, will become the structure surrounding meaningful elements of your life. Others have a different purpose—to minimize the amount of time you spend on something that needs to happen—but should take up as little space as possible in your bucket.

24 Suttida Yang, "50 Inspirational Quotes of Black Entrepreneurs & Leaders," *Suttida Yang* (blog), June 11, 2020.

25 Laura Gale, email message, November 27, 2020.

Many entrepreneurs use a lot of creative energy on projects that don't deserve it. They can spend hours every month on invoicing—using different systems, tracking everything manually, and often doing custom pricing or payment schedules for each client. A streamlined simple system can eliminate most of this work. I spend about five minutes each month on invoicing, and that's plenty. Getting paid matters, but invoicing itself doesn't deserve substantial time or problem-solving skills.

Each entrepreneur will have a different idea of where they want to channel their creativity. For instance, fashion as a creative expression isn't a priority for some entrepreneurs—they may benefit by deciding on one signature look and never changing it. For others, fashion is important, and they may set up systems to help them design creative outfits that bring them joy throughout the day. The bottom line is this—when you pinpoint the things where creativity isn't helpful, start thinking about ways to decide once, lock in your decision, and stop reinventing the wheel every time.

This can look like:

- Onboarding your clients using a single, automated process
- Saving templates you can use to answer frequently asked questions
- Using a bookkeeping tool to sync with your bank rather than manually entering all your expenses
- Planning your week in advance so you're not losing time throughout the week deciding what to do next

- Setting up a calendar tool to eliminate the back-and-forth around planning meetings

Simple systems lend themselves perfectly to checklists, standard operating procedures (SOPs), and automation. If something goes wrong, you can usually find exactly where the process broke down and determine a clear solution. Well-defined simple systems will give you much more energy to navigate the complicated and complex systems in your life.

TRY TROUBLESHOOTING AT THE SIMPLE SYSTEM LEVEL—BUT BE CAREFUL

Our biggest problems live at the complex system level. When you feel like something is broken in your business, it can cause you a lot of pain, but it will be hard to get a clear picture of what is wrong or how to fix it. Complex systems are just that—they're complex. It can be tough to peel apart the layers to diagnose exactly what is going wrong.

Simple systems have an impact at the complex system level, and oftentimes that impact can far outstrip what it seems like they should do. So, when something isn't healthy in one of your complex systems, you can sometimes use simple systems to move in the direction of a resolution.

At one point in my business, I felt really "off." I wasn't getting the results I wanted from my marketing, and it weighed heavily on me. I was discouraged, and for the first time in years, I thought about quitting. I knew a variety of challenges were contributing to my situation: my faith life, my mindset, my physical energy, and of course, my marketing strategy, skills, and consistency. There was also a big question mark over my offer itself—I knew it probably wasn't the problem, but I wasn't certain.

I realized if I stayed stuck in the complexities of my situation, I would become increasingly disheartened and make little progress. So, I started to set up simple systems to break down the problem and address it:

- I read through a list of important principles and affirmations every morning to stay grounded
- I met with a counselor twice a month
- I tracked the marketing metrics I could control and followed a single strategy
- I set aside extra time for ten weeks to break out from my rut
- I invested in marketing experts to help me move forward more effectively

Did the problem evaporate? No, it did not. But each one of these things had a clear, positive impact on my business and mindset. Over time, my hard work began to pay off through my revenue and clients.

"A complex system that works is invariably found to have evolved from a simple system that worked."

—JOHN GALL

When a complex system isn't working, its scope and interconnectedness can paralyze us. Simple systems give us the opportunity to find a clear starting point and build from there. Just as it's easier to steer a moving car, it's easier to diagnose a complex problem by starting where we can and digging deeper as we go. We have to be careful, though, to avoid using a simple system as a Band-Aid over a complex problem and then congratulating ourselves for "fixing it" and walking away.

Starting with a simple system doesn't get us off the hook—we still need to do the deeper work of understanding how the pieces work together, where the root problem is, and how we can address it long term. As Rafiq Elmansy, a professor of Design Thinking in Cairo, explains: "All systems are composed of interconnected parts, and changing one part affects the entire system, including other parts... System behavior is hard to predict due its continuously changing, nonlinear relations and its time delay. It can't be predicted by simply inspecting its elements or structure."[26] If you have a water leak in your house, putting a bucket under the drip is a great first step, but we all know you shouldn't stop there. If we're reckless with our simple systems, we can end up doing more harm than good, so we need to respect the interconnectedness of our systems and proceed with care.

***

There's a bit of a paradox in your simple systems—their impact runs deep, but you don't want to spend too much time on them. When you find a way to cut out simple systems that don't serve you, streamline the necessary but burdensome

---

26 Rafiq Elmansy, "The Six Systems Thinking Steps to Solve Complex Problems," *Designorate* (blog), February 9, 2016.

ones, and cultivate the ones that build health in your complex systems, you'll be well on your way toward an aligned business (and life).

KEY TAKEAWAYS FROM CHAPTER 3:

- Simple systems may be straightforward, but they are often far from easy or automatic.
- You can cultivate simple systems to support the complex systems that mean the most to you.
- Wherever you can, lock your simple systems into automations, habits, and routines so your energy can be focused where you need it most.
- If something is wrong with a complicated or complex system, take a moment to look at the simple systems that support it. It's often easier to troubleshoot at this level, but be careful not to call it quits with a Band-Aid solution without going deeper and understanding the root causes and the most effective response.

CONTINUE READING TO LEARN ABOUT THE COMPLICATED SYSTEMS IN YOUR LIFE.

QUESTIONS FOR REFLECTION AND DISCUSSION:

1. What's a routine or habit that you've always meant to build? What systems can you set up in your life to help you build that habit?
2. Are there areas of your life or business where you use a lot of creative energy and reinvent the wheel, but you know you're not getting much benefit from that effort? Where can you lock in a single system instead?

3. What are some simple systems you could try out for the express purpose of strengthening a complex system (like your marriage, your relationship with a dear friend, or your health)?

CHAPTER 4

HOW COMPLICATED SYSTEMS WORK

"If you can't describe what you are doing as a process, you don't know what you are doing."

—W. EDWARDS DEMING

If you've ever thought you needed to get some "processes and systems" in place, you were probably thinking about your complicated systems. The operational structures that make up how you find clients, serve them, and run your business are complicated—they're a sequence of simple systems that work together to achieve a single result. When your complicated systems are inefficient, you're going to feel it immediately. Big projects will feel daunting, you'll find yourself putting out fires every day, and you'll spend far too much time deciding what to do next.

When our clients first come to my company—A Squared Online—for help, they often describe major problems in their complicated systems. They spend hours creating proposals and onboarding new clients, have no way to track their revenue and expenses, or lose track of things they meant to do. Teams who don't have effective ways to work together will lose time trying to figure out what's going on, tracking down lost documents, or duplicating each other's work. It's not fun for anyone.

Think of your complicated system like a water pipeline, with a sequence of metal pipes soldered together. When all the pieces are connected and streamlined, water flows through it without any resistance. But what happens when a piece of pipe is missing, or you have a convoluted maze of pipes that go all over the place with no rhyme or reason? Most of the water coming through the pipeline won't reach its intended destination.

"Complicated systems have many moving parts, but they operate in patterned ways... It's possible to make accurate predictions about how a complicated system will behave. For instance, flying a commercial airplane involves complicated but predictable steps, and as a result it's astonishingly safe."[27]

—GÖKÇE SARGUT AND RITA GUNTHER MCGRATH

Your business works in the same way. When you think of your process as a step-by-step sequence that moves your project through the pipeline, it becomes easier to design. It may

---

27 Gökçe Sargut and Rita Gunther McGrath, "Learning to Live with Complexity," *Harvard Business Review*, September 2011.

be a complicated system, but the simpler and more streamlined it becomes, the better off you are.

As you start working with your complicated systems, there are four things to keep in mind: Define your complicated systems, utilize the right buckets for your projects, prepare for your systems to become invisible, and don't simply mimic the systems used by others.

CAPTURE AND DEFINE YOUR COMPLICATED SYSTEMS

A variety of complicated systems exist in your business. Some of them might be unique to you, but every business should have a working pipeline in the following areas:

- Customer experience
- Marketing
- Sales
- Finance
- Leadership

If you're running a business, you have a system for these things already. You might not have them perfectly documented or consciously designed, but if you have happy customers and are getting paid, something's there. All you need are the tools and confidence to see your processes clearly and strengthen them over time.

Mike Michalowicz, a seasoned entrepreneur and best-selling author, published a book called *Clockwork: Design Your*

Business to Run Itself in 2018.[28] He dedicated an entire chapter to the process of capturing systems and did us all a favor by upending the traditional understanding of what it means to create an SOP (Standard Operating Procedure). He said, "You have every single system for your business already. Every single stinking thing...You already follow a process, in your head. So you don't need to create anything new...The goal is not to create systems; the goal is to capture systems—and do it easily."[29] Michalowicz suggests using a screen recording tool to record a process as it's happening rather than painstakingly writing out the steps. For example, if you're loading data into a software tool, you can press record before you start and talk through what's happening as you go. In doing so, you can download what's in your head, and updating the system later is as simple as recording a new video.[30]

Once you've captured your system as it exists today, you can start to solve for any pain points you might be experiencing. Most of your business problems originate in your systems, so understanding your process will enable you to trace back to the real problem and fix it.

Caroline Mays is a brilliant bio writer. She reached out to me when she was having a problem that most of us dream to have but find miserable when we experience it—she was booked out for a year and getting new prospects through the door on a daily basis. She was reinventing the wheel for every client

---

28 Mike Michalowicz, *Clockwork: Design Your Business to Run Itself* (New York: Portfolio, 2018), 107.

29 Ibid.

30 Ibid.

and struggled to keep up with invoicing, onboarding, and setting expectations with her clients. She hated this part of the process and wanted to spend as little time managing her projects as possible. She just wanted to dig into her clients' stories and write.

Caroline was experiencing a problem with her customer experience system. The process we followed together to get her streamlined pipeline flowing is the same one you can follow with your own complicated systems:

- **We wrote down, step by step, what needed to happen** in her business, starting with the moment a potential client reached out to her and ending with a post-project testimonial. We talked about invoicing, contracts, setting expectations, making her clients feel special, and everything she needed to gather to start the project.
- **We added in a few pieces** that she always wanted to include, like a fun welcome email to help her clients know what to expect.
- **We created email templates** to capture her unique voice while automating the process.
- **We set up a software tool** that she could use to send an invoice and contract in a matter of seconds.
- **We tested the process with a fake client** to make sure everything was working and to build her confidence.
- **We created a simple checklist** she could use to remember the process going forward or delegate it to someone else.

The process was a bit painful for Caroline. She wasn't used to thinking about her customer experience this way, and she didn't enjoy having to slow down and walk through each step systematically with me. But once we had everything rolling, she was thrilled to discover she could focus all her energy on her writing. When she described the difference, she said, "My admin load will be a fraction of what it was because I have benefited from the genius of Ashlee Berghoff, who is some kind of Moses, parting the sea to create a clear path through my admin/system/to-dos I was drowning in. I cannot believe how streamlined my system is now any more than I can believe I just made a biblical reference (I'm as secular as they come)."

That sigh of relief in written form is what keeps me going.

Streamlining a process in your business might not be your favorite activity, but the payoff is enormous. When you pause for a moment and make a map you can follow to get from Point A to Point B, you'll begin to see steps you can cut, elements you can automate, and shortcuts you can take to get the same outcome, faster.

GATHER RELATED ELEMENTS OF YOUR WORK INTO "BUCKETS" THAT MAKE SENSE

Imagine for a moment that you have a free afternoon and decide to make some homemade cookies. You rummage through the pantry to find some flour, head downstairs to your other pantry for chocolate chips, and then take a quick trip to the store for some eggs. Once you return, you start mixing your ingredients but then have to head back downstairs for the right spoon, pop up to the attic for your KitchenAid, and track down your baking sheet in the yard because your child was using it as a sled for her stuffed animals. How exhausting would it be if every cooking experience was like this?

Believe it or not, many of us spend our days doing the mental version of this culinary insanity—hopping around from folder to folder to get the details we need, digging into old emails to remember what a client said, and tracking our projects across a sequence of handwritten notes we keep losing. The ingredients we need to accomplish a task are scattered all over our virtual houses.

All of that bouncing has a real cost. Neuroscientist Daniel Levitin explains it this way: "We're not actually keeping a lot of balls in the air like an expert juggler; we're more like a bad amateur plate spinner, frantically switching from one task to another, ignoring the one that is not right in front of us but worried it will come crashing down any minute."[31] The cost we're paying is real, leading to anxiety, mental depletion, loss of memory and computing power, and even addiction to the quick hits of always moving to something new.

Rachel and Mary are brilliant leaders within a growing company. When we began to work together, they were juggling a team, multiple campaigns running simultaneously, and a large volume of content that needed to be published quickly and accurately across a variety of platforms. As we talked through how they spent their time, I began to hear things like this: "So, to get this email published, I need to go into this document to gather the information, then make a task over

31 Daniel J. Levitin, "Why the Modern World Is Bad for Your Brain," *The Guardian*, January 18, 2015.

here and ask that person to write it. Then I check to make sure it's written, then make another task, then update this other document, then ping this other person to review..." I was in awe of their ability to track this process as it bounced back and forth among many different locations and people, but I knew we could find a way to make their lives easier.

As I tracked the process, I began to notice their problem wasn't a lack of documentation (they had plenty) but rather how many scattered elements they had to gather to complete a single task. Rather than all their cooking tools being in the kitchen, they were stored throughout the house.

For instance, their campaign planning document looked like this:

Campaigns

- Half-off promo
- Live event
- Course launch

Tools needed

- Webinar for the live event
- New landing page for the course launch
- Email sequence for the half-off promo

Promos

- Early bird discount for the live event
- Referral bonus for the course launch

Even in this simple example, you're probably trying to match which discount goes with which campaign and which tool. When the team sat down to work, they would try to work on each campaign individually, but had to pull data from several places to do so. Their project management tool had the same challenge—the same task would live at various times in different projects because they were bucketing by categories that didn't match how they worked.

When we s things up, the marketing director was able to plan out each campaign as a single unit:

Live event campaign

- Description
- Tools
- Promos

The team saved time on tracking an item all the way through the process, but more importantly, they were able to save the mental energy they had been using to reprocess information into the right categories.

In your own business, think about how you work. How do you want to think about each project in your business? What are the units you want to use? How often do you have to bounce to several different places to get the information you need? Once you know that, you'll be able to organize information and your process in the right way.

This same concept can be used to help you combine smaller tasks into a single block—a process called "batching"—so you can make focused progress in one direction rather than switching from task to task to task (which drastically reduces your brain's effectiveness). In my business, a core element of my marketing process is being active and engaged on LinkedIn. I post daily, have conversations, and engage with the content others share. I could split these projects up into three different units, or have LinkedIn open all day so I can respond quickly as things pop up. But both options would require me to do more bouncing into and out of LinkedIn than I want to do, and boundless projects could eat up my time for deep work. Instead, I set aside one hour each day to dedicate my focus to LinkedIn. It matches the way I work and protects the rest of my day for things like writing or program development.

PREPARE FOR YOUR SYSTEMS TO BECOME INVISIBLE

My biggest pet peeve about systems is that when they work, they become invisible. We don't spend much time thinking about how useful it is to have a thumb, or how easy it is to order something with two clicks of a mouse and then have it appear on our doorstep. We don't talk at the dinner table regularly about how grateful we are that we can turn on a tap and get an abundant supply of fresh water.

We tend to only notice systems when they break. When a pipe bursts in our basement, or we cut our thumb and can't use it, or COVID-19 disrupts our supply chain at Amazon, then that system becomes very visible to us. If you think about the systems in your business, it's natural for you to pay the most attention to the ones that aren't working well.

My guess, though, is that you're already using systems that *do* work for you. If you're still feeling like systems might not be for you, or you're just not good at them, I challenge you to take a moment right now to bring into your attention the systems in your business that are humming along. Does your inbox consistently receive messages? Have you shown up for your scheduled calls today? Did you meet a deadline last week? Are you getting consistent sleep, or keeping a pot of flowers alive?

> *"Good design, when it's done well, becomes invisible. It's only when it's done poorly that we notice it."*
>
> —JARED SPOOL

Once you realize you are already using systems effectively and they're just invisible, you'll feel more encouraged to add a few more streamlined systems to that list. Just be ready to only notice your progress in hindsight, when you look back and remember how stressed out you *used* to be.

AVOID MIMICKING THE COMPLICATED SYSTEMS OF YOUR PEERS WITHOUT CONSIDERING YOUR UNIQUE PERSONALITY AND NEEDS

I've noticed a trend among entrepreneurs that I like to call "software FOMO." The conversation goes something like this:

Entrepreneur: So I got this workflow tool because my friend Shawn said it's amazing for his business.

Me: Oh sure! How is that working for you?

Entrepreneur: I don't use it at all. It makes no sense to me.

Me: [Asks a sequence of questions to understand what's going on]. So, it sounds like you don't need that tool—you need to define your systems and then use something like this other one instead.

Entrepreneur: And that one will solve all my problems, right?

Me: No. Unfortunately, every software tool has gaps and trade-offs. I wish I could tell you they don't. It will help you, but there will be some things you don't like.

Entrepreneur: I thought with so many tools out there, something had to exist that would check all the boxes.

Me: You'd think so, but no.

I hate being the bearer of bad news, but the counterintuitive truth is that conversations like this ultimately help entrepreneurs feel better. When they go down the rabbit hole on a quest for a process or a software tool that will fix everything, they constantly feel like the system they use might be the wrong one. They're always keeping one eye open for something better and comparing themselves to others. But once they realize their dream tool doesn't exist and what works for them might be different than what works for their peers, it becomes much easier to settle down.

It's kind of like dating, really. If you're always wondering if someone better is out there even when you're with someone great, prepare for some online dating-driven misery!

***

Strong complicated systems will remove a lot of the friction in your business and allow you to maximize the progress you get from each step you take. When you can see the systems at work in your business and know how to put the puzzle pieces in place, you'll find yourself turning more and more of your creative ideas into reality.

KEY TAKEAWAYS FROM CHAPTER 4:

- Complicated systems bring a variety of simple systems together to accomplish an outcome.
- Trying to hold your complicated systems in your head will lead to dropped balls and a lot of headaches (not to mention making it hard to delegate). It's worth the time to document and define how your business systems work.
- As you define your complicated systems, think about how you naturally work and think. If you tend to do things together, make sure those elements are bucketed together so you're not bouncing from place to place.
- Great systems are invisible. Be ready for this.
- Imitation isn't always the best idea with your systems. Feel free to learn from your peers, but be sure to customize their methods for your own situation.

CONTINUE READING TO LEARN ABOUT THE TRICKIEST SYSTEMS OF ALL—YOUR COMPLEX SYSTEMS.

QUESTIONS FOR REFLECTION AND DISCUSSION:

1. If you found yourself hospitalized for a few weeks, what would happen in your business? Would anyone else be able to keep the core systems running?
2. Are you often tempted to prematurely abandon your systems for the solutions you see around you?
3. Are there areas where you find yourself bouncing from place to place to get a single task done (think different folders, different data sources, or even different physical locations)? Where can you bring things together to add more efficiency?

CHAPTER 5

HOW COMPLEX SYSTEMS WORK

"Today the network of relationships linking the human race to itself and to the rest of the biosphere is so complex that all aspects affect all others to an extraordinary degree."

—MURRAY GELL-MANN

Complex systems aren't just the culmination of all the simple and complicated systems in our lives. They're the whole reason we have those systems in the first place.

Thomas Edison didn't invent the lightbulb simply to prove there was a way to channel electricity and make light. His invention, in itself a simple system, revolutionized human life. The way we work, live, and play is different now. Our simple and complicated systems should do the same thing by contributing to health in our complex systems. When they do, they will have an outsized impact on the quality and even the length of our lives.

I started my business (a complex system) because of how I wanted my life (another complex system) to look. As I prepared to graduate with an MBA, I began to feel the tension between the path mapped out for us and the family my husband and I wanted to have. My classmates, both men and women, were navigating the same challenges, saying:

"I want to be present with my family *and* have a fulfilling career."

"My job makes it hard for me to step away from work."

"It's exhausting to juggle everything going on at work and home."

I was frustrated that my options were expressed as a dichotomy. I could either quit my job when my child arrived and stay home with her, or I could work a full-time job away from home. In between, I saw a thousand multilevel marketing schemes and a few coveted flexible jobs, but not much else.

Without knowing it at the time, I was longing for a single integrated complex system that contained *both* a business that challenged me *and* the freedom to mold that business around the needs of our family. I didn't want a tug of war—I wanted my work to strengthen my home, and I wanted my home to complement my work.

Becoming a leader in the context of an entrepreneurial business has given me the ability to build that kind of life for myself, but the impact has extended further than I anticipated. Even in a small business, I find myself at the helm of systems that have a powerful impact on other people. Other people depend on me for their livelihood. My business has an impact on our industry, and the content I create could have a ripple effect far beyond what I can see. As a business owner, I am responsible for these impacts and for the legacy I leave behind.

When I first defined and addressed systems, I used a macro view of the larger systems of culture, government, and society to demonstrate the power of systems. If you're an entrepreneur, you might feel like you don't have a direct impact on systems like those, and you're right—many of the systems we live in are beyond our full control. But we are responsible for the systems we build and how we contribute to the larger systems around us.

Through my research and conversations with entrepreneurs, I identified five principles we can use to steward this responsibility effectively and build valuable, healthy systems: define your purpose, use systems to protect your values, remind yourself of your biggest priorities, don't expect arrival, and share the purpose of your systems with others.

START WITH YOUR WHY—DEFINE THE PURPOSE OF YOUR SYSTEMS

When a system aligns with our values, we can channel its power in the right direction. In contrast, the wrong systems can take us away from our deeper Why. If we follow a business strategy simply because it is more lucrative or work too much out of pure habit, we can become our own worst enemies. Our career arcs and businesses are complex systems; if we set up systems without thinking about what we want our legacy to be, processes can become the wall between us and the things we value most. They can stifle our creativity, force us to operate in a way that doesn't work for us, or cause inadvertent damage to our teams or clients. But when we know what matters most to us and what we want our businesses to accomplish, we can build systems that turn our visions into reality.

When I started my business, I was thinking mostly about the lifestyle I wanted to build. There was nothing wrong with that, but as I learned more about my industry and the incredible clients I worked with, a deeper vision began to emerge. I felt a deep sense of connection to lifestyle-driven entrepreneurs—freelancers and former freelancers who started their business for more freedom, just like I did. I began to realize that many of them weren't experiencing freedom at all. When they were working, they worried about whether they were missing something important. When they weren't working, they felt guilty and wondered if everything was falling apart. I wanted to use my skill set to build some solid ground under their feet. When opportunities arose for me to raise my prices and work with larger companies, I chose to adjust my business model instead to continue working with these people.

Meanwhile, my team started to grow, and I realized I had another opportunity—to create amazing, flexible, part-time jobs for other people. I had started this business to create a great part-time career for myself, but I had the chance to be part of a much broader solution in the changing world of work. Piece by piece, I started to build a different type of culture for A Squared. From bringing on W-2 employees in an industry where contractors are the norm, to providing paid sick leave when a team member contracted COVID, to giving raises as quickly as I could afford to, I made my vision for our team a priority. My efforts were imperfect and are still ongoing, but I found ways to turn my vision into tangible systems in the business.

"Vocation is the place where our deep gladness meets the world's deep need."

—FREDERICK BUECHNER

In Okinawa, Japan, a prevalent ideology has been credited for the long and healthy lives of many of its residents. The ideology is called "ikigai" (pronounced EE-key-guy), which translates to "reason for being."[32] In Okinawa, people are taught to cultivate a sense of meaning and purpose in their lives and work. To do this, they look for the intersection of things they love, things they are good at, and things their world needs.[33] Studies show that in addition to diet, exercise, and genetic factors, a sense of ikigai is a critical component of a long and healthy life.[34]

---

32 Héctor García and Francesc Miralles, *Ikigai: The Japanese Secret to a Long and Happy Life* (New York: Penguin, 2016).

33 Ken Mogi, "This Japanese Secret to a Longer and Happier Life Is Gaining Attention from Millions Around the World," *CNBC*, May 22, 2019.

34 García and Miralles, *Ikigai.*

To cultivate ikigai in your own life and business, take some time to dig deeper into your values. What do you want *your* life to look like? What matters most to you? Are the systems in your business building toward the life you want, or are they taking you in a different direction?

Asking these questions will help you identify your values and the systems you want to build from them. They also create space for quieter voices in your mind to have a say. In their book about the principles of ikigai, Hector Garcia and Francesc Miralles write, "Our intuition and curiosity are very powerful internal compasses to help us connect with our ikigai."[35] Understanding your values can take a lifetime, and you may want to talk through these questions with others as you think about them, but you don't need a perfect understanding to move forward with greater depth.

Once you begin to be in tune with your values, you'll be able to make specific choices about how those values will play out in your work. Your business is a complex system, so you won't be able to find one "right answer," but you can make honest choices about what you will do and why. Training yourself to think deeply about your values is difficult, and you'll need to revisit them repeatedly, but when you're building something as powerful as a system, it's worth the work.

If you have a team, the same principle applies. Knowing your values and strategies and communicating them effectively to your team will help your business operate in line with your Why. Layering processes onto the team without keeping

---

35 Ibid.

those priorities in mind will lead to inefficiency, frustration, and an outcome far afield of your true target.

In 2001, a group of software professionals hailing from a variety of different industry philosophies met to ski together and search for common ground. They all had their own ideas of how new technologies should be created, but they agreed on one thing—their industry had lost its commitment to a shared sense of purpose. The drive for innovation had compelled many companies to lose sight of their team members and customers. Together, the group came up with the Agile Manifesto, a set of principles about iteration and team building that has since transformed the working styles of thousands of businesses. "At the core, I believe Agile Methodologists are really about 'mushy' stuff," said Jim Highsmith, a member of the Agile Alliance.[36] "[It's] about delivering good products to customers by operating in an environment that does more than talk about 'people as our most important asset' but actually 'acts' as if people were the most important, and loses the word 'asset.'"[37]

People who commit to the Agile style of working choose to value people over process and iteration over commitment to a plan. Planning and processes are good things, but they can cause a lot of damage when the purpose isn't kept front and center.[38] Once you've planted a flag in your values and return to them often, you're ready to build systems that protect those values.

---

36 Jim Highsmith, "History: The Agile Manifesto," The Agile Alliance, 2001.

37 Ibid.

38 "Manifesto for Agile Software Development," The Agile Alliance, 2001.

BUILD SYSTEMS TO PROTECT YOUR VALUES, EVEN WHEN YOU CAN'T CONTROL ALL THE ELEMENTS

No matter what you do, some things will be out of your control. Your body will continue to need regular meals whether you like it or not, and many rhythms in your life will involve other people and their own values. But when you clarify the systems in your life and recognize where you have autonomy to design them, you can decide what structure your life should take and where you need extra protection.

We often use the word "protect" liberally, but I've thought a lot lately about what that word means. Protection is, by nature, about conflict and being willing to fight. For example, if you protect something, you are by definition protecting it *from* a force that would do it harm. So, if you're protecting your values, what or who are you protecting them *from*? If you're anything like me, it could be yourself. Protecting your ikigai might mean setting up structures to protect yourself from workaholic habits, or a tendency toward perfectionism. Or, it might look like adding some structure to help you work out consistently or limit your time on social media. You might not be able to change your habits overnight, but you can put things in place to protect your values, even from your own bad habits.

When I made the choice to build my work systems around a part-time schedule, I thought I would immediately feel a deep sense of connection and meaning to my new way of living in the world. But it wasn't that simple. I sometimes envied my husband's eight hours of focused work time or got frustrated when my team wouldn't complete a project in the same way

I would have done it. It was easy to notice others growing their businesses more quickly with their extra availability.

But now, looking back at the first year of my daughter's life, I remember a whole lot less about those projects I cared so much about. I remember my daughter's face, though. I remember how much she loved bath time, and how it felt when she started to laugh for the first time. If left to my own devices, I would've missed more of her first year than I intended to without realizing it. My system couldn't fully protect me from myself, but it went a long way toward helping me keep my eyes on what mattered most to me.

REMIND YOURSELF REGULARLY OF YOUR BIGGEST PRIORITIES

It would be great if we naturally stayed attuned to what matters most in our lives, but the truth is that we don't. We are easily distracted, and what's in front of our faces often keeps our attention better than investing in our deepest values. Systems built for what matters are so valuable because they can keep you on track, even when your own focus on your values waxes and wanes.

Not only can you have systems that protect your values, but you can also have systems to remind you of them. Many entrepreneurs follow a morning ritual to center their minds on their vision and goals, and you'll also see this same sort of memory exercise in faith practices. Arianna Huffington starts each day with deep breathing and at least twenty minutes of meditation before doing anything else.[39] The sixteenth century theologian, Martin Luther, famously said, "I have so much to do that I shall spend the first three hours in prayer."[40]

I have a vision board on my wall with eight pictures capturing things that matter to me in my business, including Monica Aldana from *Cheer*, to remind me how I want to show up as a coach for my team, and an image of a group of friends at a scenic overlook, to capture my dream of taking my team on annual adventure retreats together. I have pictures capturing what I want our business to mean for the local community, how I want to show up as a woman, wife, and mother, and my dream of someday buying land and owning horses again.

You can set up similar systems in your own life, or even post your deepest values in your office where you see them every day. Don't trust yourself to stay the course—allow your systems to work with you to keep your vision clear.

DON'T EXPECT "ARRIVAL"—COMPLEX SYSTEMS ARE DYNAMIC AND EVER CHANGING

As you gain clarity on your values and set up systems to protect them, be careful not to anticipate a shining, glorious moment when you have "arrived." You'll have encouragement along the way, and empowerment, and a deep sense of

---

39 Garik Tate, "Arianna Huffington Talks Meditation, the Importance of Failure, and the Underrated Power of Sleep," *High Existence*, accessed March 3, 2021.

40 Andrew Haslam, "Luther's Advice: Concentrate When You Pray," *Think*, September 10, 2015.

meaning, but your life is too dynamic for arrival. You will never stop changing, and your systems will need to adjust along with those changes. Meanwhile, you'll never be able to reduce a complex system to its component parts, see every connection, or trace a clear line of cause and effect.

Complex systems are never perfect, and there will always be more work to do. It can feel like a game of Whac-A-Mole when the work you do causes downstream impacts you didn't expect, or fixing something in one area of your business ends up causing problems in another area. Building healthy systems is an ongoing process of iteration and experimentation, and expecting an easy fix will discourage you. But when you work on the roots of your systems with the understanding that you're building a healthy organism with room for improvement rather than a flawless machine, you'll have a better chance at long-term endurance. The changes you make won't be flashy, but they'll last.

Each phase of your business will have its own gifts and challenges. Times of struggle don't necessarily mean you're doing something wrong, and systems can't eliminate every challenge, but they can be tools you use to add strength and resilience to your life.

SHARE THE DEEPER PURPOSE OF YOUR SYSTEMS WITH EVERYONE IMPACTED BY THEM

"Because I said so." Every child has heard this phrase before and hated it with every fiber of their being. If we think about it, most adults hear the same phrase regularly from their bosses. It's tempting to assert our authority when explaining the deeper reason for something can feel like an arduous undertaking or a waste of time. We all know a three-year-old might not have the context to understand why they shouldn't touch a hot stove, but I hope we have more faith in our teams, spouses, and partners. When we explain what our systems are and why they matter to us, we create the opportunity for others to support us and ensure our systems actually work.

"It's a fact of life that progress is almost exclusively generated through people. If you're not sensitive to the needs of people within your organization, or with whom you have to deal, you're not going to be effective."

—REGINALD F. LEWIS

As a leader, providing transparency around your business's complex systems is critical. It gives your team the opportunity to commit more deeply to the mission and trust your guidance, and it forces you to articulate the deeper purpose within your systems. You may think you understand your systems or their ultimate outcomes, but the exercise of putting your ideas into words will get you closer to a true recognition of how your systems work and where they can be improved. Meanwhile, input from others will help you avoid unintentional negative impacts and cultivate systems that are beneficial for everyone.

***

Your life, health, relationships, beliefs, and business are all complex systems. When you take the time to recognize what matters most to you in each area of your life and channel systems to protect those values, the impact will be revolutionary. Complex systems may be messy, dynamic, and unpredictable, but you have more power than you think.

KEY TAKEAWAYS FROM CHAPTER 5:

- Your complex systems are the bedrock of everything else—they're the reason why you do anything at all.
- First and foremost, you need to understand what matters most to you. From there, you can build systems to protect your values.
- Don't trust yourself to remember your priorities. Remind yourself regularly.
- When it comes to your complex systems, prepare for a constant sense that things could be better or different. Arrival does not exist.
- Other people are impacted by your complex systems. Talk to them about what your systems are and why they matter.

CONTINUE READING TO DIVE DEEPER INTO WHY SYSTEMS GET SUCH A BAD RAP AND WHAT WE CAN DO ABOUT IT.

QUESTIONS FOR REFLECTION AND DISCUSSION:

1. What do you want your life to look like? What matters to you?
2. Where do your values need the most protection? Where are external or internal forces pulling you away from your biggest priorities?
3. How can you communicate your values and priorities with the people in your life who are most impacted by them?

CHAPTER 6

WHY WE HATE SYSTEMS

"A bad system will beat a good person every time."

—W. EDWARDS DEMING

As part of the research for this book, I interviewed an incredible woman who has spent over twenty years supporting the growth of creative entrepreneurs. Part of her work is building the infrastructure start-up founders need to succeed, but when I shared my thesis with her that systems are a critical part of entrepreneurship, she pushed back. "I've seen brilliant artists build incredible businesses without paying that much attention to systems," she said. Since most of us naturally think of systems as process maps and checklists rather than the structure under our lives and the disciplines that fueled history's greatest artists, I didn't blame her.

Later that week, I told my writing group about my book and about how fascinated I am by processes and systems. "Every time my boss comes out with a new process for us to follow, we all groan and roll our eyes," one of them said. "It was always a bunch of extra unnecessary stuff we had to do that made our lives harder. They never talked to us about what we really needed."

If you think systems are ineffective, wasteful, restrictive, or unnecessary, there's a real reason you think that way. Every one of us has been inconvenienced, ignored, or even actively hurt by a bad system. One of the most poignant examples of systems gone wrong occurred in August of 2020, when an explosion rocked the city of Beirut, injuring thousands and killing over 130 people. Early suspicions pointed to a firecracker warehouse, but it quickly became evident that thousands of pounds of explosive ammonium nitrate had been stored unsafely by the government in that port since 2013. Despite many warnings from customs officials, nothing had been done.[41]

Many entrepreneurs leave the corporate world to escape red tape and bureaucracy. Not only have I worked with dozens of them, but I *am* one of them. I wanted the autonomy and flexibility to pivot quickly and grow on my own terms.

As my own business grows, I've thought a lot about what goes wrong when systems go bad, and how we can still leverage the power of systems without falling into the same traps. How can we amplify our impact without falling victim to drudgery, limiting our creative energy, or losing sight of what matters?

---

41 Jessie Yeung and Luke McGee, "What We Know about the Beirut Blast," *CNN*, August 6, 2020.

WHAT GOES WRONG (AND HOW TO MAKE THINGS GO RIGHT INSTEAD)

Three main pitfalls can impact you when you're trying to build your processes and systems: shallow solutions, not involving stakeholders, and expressing a desire while ignoring the system. If you pay attention to these potential problems, you can make design systems that improve your life.

PITFALL ONE: SOLVING SYMPTOMS INSTEAD OF THE ROOT CAUSE, OR CHOOSING A TOO SHALLOW SOLUTION

Imagine for a moment that you tend to stay up too late at night, and you know it's impacting your productivity. Maybe you end up in a political argument with your uncle on Facebook, or go down a YouTube rabbit hole, or yell at Netflix every time it asks you if you're still watching (you are, and you don't appreciate the judgmental tone).

You dream of waking up well rested every morning and diving into a big creative project that's been on your mind for months. On the rare days you get everything done you hoped to get done, you feel unstoppable. You want to feel that way more often, but you regularly need a strong cup of coffee to muster enough energy to answer your emails.

You Google "how to go to bed on time" and read a series of generic blog posts about evening routines. You try every suggestion, but nothing sticks. The shame starts to build, with the voice in your head calling you lazy, undisciplined, and addicted to technology.

What if the reason a bedtime routine doesn't fix your situation is that a lack of routine wasn't your problem in the first place? What if it's something deeper?

For many people, distraction in a situation like this isn't the problem—it's simply a symptom. If you pummel yourself with impossible expectations for daily output and productivity, or if you've said yes to too many things that drain the life out of you, or if every day you face a daunting challenge you can't seem to overcome, it's likely that you stay up late to avoid having to go to sleep and then wake up to a day like that.

If that's you, bedtime systems won't help you. But you know what might? Looking squarely at those expectations and challenges and shifting them. Human-sizing your expectations for yourself, saying no, and getting the help you need might start making it much easier to face each day and go to bed each night exactly when you want to.

> *"Whatever you are not changing, you are choosing."*
>
> —LAURIE BUCHANAN[42]

This same problem happens in businesses too. Let's say your team is experiencing a lot of chaos and stress in a major recurring project for your business. Everyone is juggling a ton of moving pieces, and things fall through the cracks regularly. You ask your favorite Facebook group what to do,

---

42 Laurie Buchanan, "Tuesdays with Laurie," *Tuesdays with Laurie* (blog), last updated November 24, 2020.

and several people say you need to document things, or you need to make an SOP (Standard Operating Procedure). So, you ask a junior team member to spend time documenting step by step everything that's happening. That person does their best to capture the process, but they fall even further behind because it takes so long. Six months later, the process they wrote is now out of date and no one is using it.

What went wrong? In both examples, the attempted solution doesn't work for one reason—the real problem is still sitting beneath the surface, utterly unfazed by the changes you're trying to make. It's like taking ibuprofen to solve your broken bone. Cutting the pain isn't a bad idea, but you'll want to make sure you set that bone, too. We have to be willing to go deeper.

Professors Jim Ollhoff and Michael Walcheski, in their article in *The Systems Thinker*, give eight helpful clues to know when our problem is a symptom of something deeper:

1. The problem seems too small for the amount of discussion it's causing (for example, if a team member is freaking out about something that normally wouldn't bother them, something else may be wrong)
2. The problem is easy to solve on its face, but people aren't solving it
3. The problem won't go away
4. The problem involves emotional barriers—people are unwilling to think about change in this area
5. The problem has a pattern
6. Your company is keeping the problem around, like a pet

7. Everyone is in a state of stress or anxiety
8. Solving one problem leads to another one[43]

You need to take systems seriously because they are so powerful and complex. One way you can do that is by thinking much more deeply about your systems before launching off into a solution. You can write down your current processes to understand what's happening, but you shouldn't see documentation as a solution on its own. It's too shallow of a solution because if your process is broken, codifying it won't do a single thing to fix it. It's like writing down a recipe for a meal you hate. Instead, you need to get your process working. *Then* you can lock in an SOP. By "working," I mean this: does it achieve the intended outcome efficiently and effectively? Does everyone in the team have what they need to get it done consistently?

Following these steps will help you solve the right problem:

- Write down what is happening today (this isn't an SOP—just a way to understand how things work).
- Identify the different simple, complicated, or complex systems that are involved in your problem.
- Ask, "Where are things not working the way they should?"
- Dig deeper to identify why things are going wrong.
- Map out what you would like to see happen, step by step. If needed, start with the outcome you want and work backward. Don't just write down what's happening now—try to pinpoint what should happen instead.

---

43 Jim Ollhoff and Michael Walcheski, "Making the Jump to Systems Thinking," *The Systems Thinker*, accessed February 13, 2021.

- Think about mindset habits, lifestyle elements, or other factors that might be impacting your ability to get the outcome you want.
- Experiment with a new set of systems to help you avoid those obstacles and achieve the right result.
- Once you find something that works, document it simply (often a video recording and checklist are enough) and think about ways to automate it.

PITFALL TWO: NOT INVOLVING THE PEOPLE WHO WILL USE THE SYSTEM

When a "solution" is being shoved down our throats, we'll rebel against it. Even if we accept it, we won't own it. I learned this lesson in the early days of my business.

When I first started working with clients on process design projects, I would ask questions, design the process on my own, and bring it to my clients on a silver platter. It meant about as much to them as if I handed them an advanced piece of technology they'd never seen before. My clients were able to use their systems, but they couldn't adapt them to ongoing changes in their businesses. They loved having their problem fixed, but they didn't experience ownership over their own operations. Now, I see myself as a "systems personal trainer"—I work alongside my clients to build their muscles so they can develop and use their own systems.

Leaders in larger teams can be especially tempted to build systems independently and force them on the rest of the team. This single issue has caused a lot of the angst we tend to feel about systems. Even solo operators might build a program they think is amazing without really understanding what their ideal clients need. Any time we're building a system, we need to make sure we're capturing the people who most need to benefit from it.

In 2016, McKinsey and Company, one of the world's most famous consulting firms, studied how companies transform and found that 70 percent of complex and large-scale change programs never succeed. This means that even for large, well-funded companies, changing systems is far from easy. But what's even more important is *why* this happens. According to the study, the most important factors were "a lack of employee engagement, inadequate management support, poor or nonexistent cross-functional collaboration, and a lack of accountability."[44] Every single one of these factors has to do with the people involved and how they work together.

In the context of your own business, what is the best way to involve the right people? Here are a few puzzle pieces to keep in mind:

- Before you start fixing things, sit down with everyone who uses the system on a daily basis (whether they're your clients or your team). Ask them open-ended questions about what the problem really is. Avoid leading questions like, "wouldn't it be great if we...?"—most people are too polite to crush your dreams. Instead, you can use a helpful framework called Jobs to Be Done to ask questions about the things that determine our openness to change:

---

44 Michael Bucy et al., "The 'How' of Transformation," *McKinsey and Company*, May 9, 2016.

- What pain do you want to escape from?
- What better future are you attracted to?
- What anxieties do you have about changing?
- How connected are you to your current habits?[45]

- Pay close attention to when you are speaking for someone else rather than letting them speak for themselves. For instance, if your racial equity committee includes only white people, something is wrong.
- Notice when you might be excited about a potential solution or new system and be inclined to defend it. Excitement isn't bad, but it's important to be aware of when you might be blinded to other solutions that are ultimately more effective.
- Empower the people who use a system regularly to propose and implement solutions.

PITFALL THREE: EXPRESSING A DESIRE WITHOUT DIGGING INTO THE SYSTEM

In the documentary *The Social Dilemma*, a young tech executive named Tristan Harris talks about a presentation he created to raise the alarm about the harmful impacts of social media.[46] He was working at Google at the time, and he shared his slides with a few trusted colleagues. Within twenty-four hours, hundreds of people within Google had commented with support and agreement; they too were worried and wanted to see things change. The slide deck landed

45 Chris Spiek, "Unpacking the Progress Making Forces Diagram," *JTBD Radio* (blog), February 23, 2012.

46 Tristan Harris, *The Social Dilemma*, film, directed by Jeff Orlowski (Atlanta: Exposure Labs, 2020), streaming.

on the CEO's desk within a day. Clearly, Tristan had struck a chord, and he was hopeful to see what would happen next.

Nothing happened next. The noise died down, and people went back to work. Tristan eventually left Google to start the Center for Humane Technology, which he still leads today.[47]

When brokenness in a system finds itself in a spotlight, we are likely to express our outrage and frustration. When enough of us do that, our leaders will often step forward and promise change. They will declare that the company (or the country) will do better and they will do what it takes to keep damaging effects from happening again.

We know how that story ends. More often than not, nothing changes. At most, leaders might slap one of those shallow solutions on top of the problem with a regulation or a new process to stop the problem without digging into why it happened in the first place.

Something dangerous can happen when people are faced with this type of inaction and lack of change—they might decide to burn the whole thing down and start again. Sometimes, a fresh start is the best solution, but without a clear plan for a stronger system, the result can be counterproductive. We can, and *must*, learn how to press in and do the hard work of making real systems better.

The work of changing systems from the roots up is not sexy. It's not going to bring applause or catch peoples' eyes, and

47 Ibid.

the invisibility of effective systems means people might not even notice when the bad outcome has stopped happening. But that's where the real change happens—not on the podium in a courageous speech, but in the hard work of changing the way the system works. It can take a lot of time and consistent action, but that's how we turn the tide.

> *"From an early age we are taught to break apart problems, to fragment the world. This apparently makes complex tasks and subjects more manageable, but we pay a hidden, enormous price. We can no longer see the consequences of our actions: we lose our intrinsic sense of connection to a larger whole."*
>
> —PETER SENGE

***

Since systems are all about structure, it's a bit ironic that complex systems are so messy. They are powerful, deep, and complex, melding many different elements and having an impact far beyond what you might expect. As business owners, we can create systems that didn't exist before. When we learn how to wield that power responsibly, we can transform our own lives, our clients' lives, and the world around us. It's worth the work to take systems seriously.

KEY TAKEAWAYS FROM CHAPTER 6:

- If you hate systems, you have a good reason. Because systems are so powerful, misusing them can cause real suffering.
- Systems go wrong when you:

- Solve a symptom instead of the real cause
- Fail to involve the people most impacted by a system
- Express a desire for things to change but don't change the system

- Changing a system from the roots up isn't sexy, but that's where things change.

CONTINUE READING TO LEARN HOW SYSTEMS WILL MOVE YOU FROM YOUR FAVORITE EUREKA MOMENTS TO EXPERIENCING ACTUAL EUREKA RESULTS.

QUESTIONS FOR REFLECTION AND DISCUSSION:

1. How have you been hurt by bad systems in the past?
2. Where do you need to dig deeper into the systems of something that's not working well in your life or business?
3. Do you still feel the same way about systems that you did before you began this book?

PART TWO

PRINCIPLES OF EUREKA RESULTS

CHAPTER 7

FROM EUREKA MOMENT TO EUREKA RESULT

"If more information was the answer, then we'd all be billionaires with perfect abs."

—DEREK SIVERS

Entrepreneurs are addicted to eureka moments. We rely on mind-blowing insights and new ideas for our energy and our hope. We revel in the freedom to chase our dreams. We love the rush of feeling like we've found *the* answer. But as we've discovered, eureka isn't powerful enough to get us all the way to the finish line. We need inspiration, we need grit, *and* we need systems.

Now that we've redefined the purpose of systems, we can explore how we can use them to turn our eureka moments into reality—to navigate the journey all the way to Eureka Results.

THE EUREKA RESULTS MAP

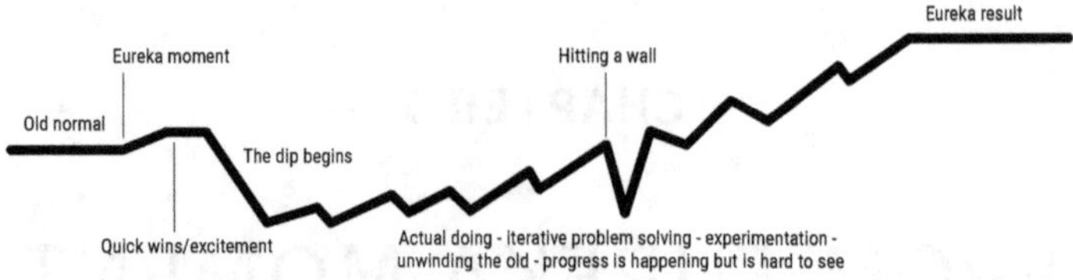

First things first—what does the journey from Eureka moment to Eureka Result even look like?

Lightbulb moments can happen to us in the strangest places. They often happen while we're actively trying to solve a problem with a coach or our entrepreneurial community, but they're just as likely to occur to us in the shower, in the middle of the night, or halfway through a game of football. No matter how they show up, our eureka moments all have one thing in common: they're full of promise for a better future. When a eureka moment comes, everything feels like it clicks into place. We've finally found the answer!

Eureka moments often give us a lot of energy, and that excitement will carry us through the first steps on our mission. We might experience some quick wins as things start to get better, and we become even more motivated to make our great idea happen.

But then, something changes. We run into our first obstacle, then our second, then our third. It's harder than we expected to break old habits. We put something out into the world, and no one notices it. We have to complete a laundry list of steps we hate to get to "the fun stuff." Resistance starts to appear, with our self-protective brain telling us to run back to safety. Discouragement and frustration might even be bad enough that we feel like we're worse off than we would have been if we'd just stayed in our old normal.

Seth Godin, one of the greatest marketing voices of our generation, calls this experience "The Dip" in his book of the same name. He describes it this way:

> "The Dip is the long slog between starting and mastery. A long slog that's actually a shortcut, because it gets you where you want to go faster than any other path...The Dip is the long stretch between beginner's luck and real accomplishment."[48]

At the point when the eureka high runs out and we find ourselves squarely in the middle of The Dip, the right systems can kick in to keep us moving forward. Practical metrics help us see progress even when we can't feel it. A system for remembering our vision keeps us from meandering down bunny trails. Operational structures free up time for creative work. After days, weeks, or even years of showing up consistently, it dawns on us—our big vision from before is our new normal now. It might look different than what we originally expected, but it's real. We've crossed the finish line for our Eureka Result.

---

48 Seth Godin, *The Dip* (New York: Portfolio, 2007), 17–18.

SYSTEMS FOR NAVIGATING THE JOURNEY

Three principles and five core systems will help you navigate the marathon between your best ideas and the outcome you envision. We will cover each one individually in the next eight chapters, but here's an itinerary so you know what to expect:

THE THREE PRINCIPLES OF EUREKA RESULTS

- To thrive as an entrepreneur, the first thing we need to do is cultivate the right expectation for the journey of turning our best ideas into reality. False optimism leads to more pain than an honest picture of what is ahead of us. When we're prepared for the long haul and know how to use systems to stay the course, we're more likely to succeed.
- Entrepreneurship is one of the most impactful personal development programs in existence, and just like every complex system, it's messy. Even as we use systems to move forward, a core principle of Eureka Results is embracing the messy middle and becoming comfortable with a constant state of change.
- The final principle of Eureka Results is to grow through action and iteration. Whether you call entrepreneurship an experiment, a journey, or an adventure, you are signing up for an endless process of learning, failure, and growth. Complex systems require an upward spiral of iterations, and embracing that process will allow you to see your progress and celebrate your imperfect but meaningful wins along the way.

CORE SYSTEMS FOR EUREKA RESULTS

- Running a great marathon is impossible if you're not on the right route in the first place. Training matters, but first and foremost, you need to run the right race. Likewise, the first core system you need in your business is a clear sense of your vision and values.
- Building a business can feel a lot more like an obstacle course than a race. You can't prevent all potholes and roadblocks, but effective planning and daily habits can help you cut out the noise so you can move forward.
- Imagine how fun a race would be if you had to change your shoes every one hundred yards, fill up your two-cup water bottle every half mile, and ask for directions constantly. At a certain point, you'd probably just stop running. You can easily see the purpose of locking systems into your personal life, but I wouldn't be surprised if you're reinventing the wheel constantly in your own business. If you're making things harder for yourself by trying to live without processes, it's time to eliminate duplicate work and make decisions once to leverage your effort.
- Once you're running the right race, fending off the distractions, and leveraging your effort, you need to see that you're making progress. A race without a finish line is torture, and running without a sense of progress will make you quit far more quickly than seeing how far you've come. You need milestones in your business.
- The final core system is leading a team who will run the race with you. Not every business will want or need this system, but if you have a vision that is bigger than yourself,

your ability to empower others with the same vision will be some of the most meaningful work you can do.

***

Mastering these systems and learning the right mindset for taking clear and focused action in your business will make you more money. More importantly, it will keep your eyes clear, your shoulders back, and your vision always in view. It will give you the strength and staying power you need to thrive at every stage of your business's journey.

KEY TAKEAWAYS FROM CHAPTER 7:

- The journey from eureka moment to Eureka Result isn't an easy one, but systems will help you get there.
- A mindset that embraces continuous iteration will give you the resilience you need to go the distance.
- You need five core systems to thrive and consistently bring your best ideas across the finish line:
  - Vision and mission
  - Effective planning and daily habits
  - Strong operational processes
  - Milestones
  - Leadership systems

CONTINUE READING TO DIVE INTO THE THREE CORE PRINCIPLES OF EUREKA RESULTS.

QUESTIONS FOR REFLECTION AND DISCUSSION:

1. Does the graphic depicting the journey from eureka moment to Eureka Result resonate with you? How has it appeared in your own life?
2. Are there any entrepreneurs who, from your perspective, were an overnight success? What do you think you might find if you dug into the details of their actual experiences?
3. What eureka moment or new idea are you most excited about turning into reality?

CHAPTER 8

CORE PRINCIPLE ONE: SETTING THE RIGHT EXPECTATIONS

"Everybody has a plan until they get punched in the mouth."

—MIKE TYSON

On the race from eureka idea to Eureka Result, it's easy to become either daunted or overly optimistic about the road in front of us. When we cultivate a fair expectation for ourselves instead, we can use systems effectively to make real progress.

The first time I saw the Incline outside of Manitou Springs in Colorado, I was blown away. In less than a mile of distance, the Incline achieves nearly two thousand feet of elevation gain. Over 2,400 stairs mark the route between the parking lot and the summit.[49] That sounds tough enough, but I've hiked it twice, and I can tell you that the roughest part isn't looking up from the parking lot at the two-thousand-foot climb. The hardest part is that you'll spend most of the hike looking at what you think is the summit, only to reach it and discover that you have another three hundred stairs to go. It's no coincidence that a well-used exit point exists right around that false summit. The final quarter is so painful not just because you're tired, but because you thought you were about to be done.

This happens to us all the time in business. False summits exist in every new milestone of growth, and it can make it hard for us to keep going. We expect that cresting six figures, or hiring our first team member, or leading a successful launch, will give us an enduring sense that we've made it. We pick some point in the future, say, "I just need to get *there*," and then set out on the climb. But when we reach the summit only to find another, steeper mountain ahead of us, our morale can tank. We may even begin to experience resentment toward anyone or anything we blame for our situation. The reality is that "there's no *there* there," as Shawn Twing, one of my favorite entrepreneurs, told me a few months ago. Each accomplishment will open doors to a new challenge, and expecting the right thing can help us avoid despair.

One of the most powerful illustrations of this concept occurs in Jim Collin's book *Good to Great* when he introduces the

---

49 "Manitou Incline: Tourist Cable Car Track Turned Heart-Pounding Workout!" Visit Colorado Springs, accessed February 15, 2021.

Stockdale Paradox.[50] Admiral James Stockdale was a prisoner of war for seven years in Vietnam. He survived brutal torture and uncertainty during the experience, but as Jim noted, he somehow managed to leave the camp stronger than when he arrived. Jim was studying leadership and success, and Admiral Stockdale's story baffled him, so he decided to ask the admiral how he managed to triumph over his ordeal. In their interview, Jim asked about what made him so resilient. Admiral Stockdale responded, "Well, you have to understand, it was never depressing. Because despite all those circumstances, I never ever wavered in my absolute faith that not only would I prevail—get out of this—but I would also prevail by turning it into the defining event of my life that would make me a stronger and better person."[51]

Admiral Stockdale's complete confidence stunned Jim, but there was another piece to the puzzle that surprised him even more. Stockdale continued, "I can tell you who didn't make it out. It was the optimists...They were the ones who said, 'We're going to be out by Christmas.' And Christmas would come, and Christmas would go. Then they'd say, 'We're going to be out by Easter.' And Easter would come, and Easter would go. And then Thanksgiving, and then it would be Christmas again. And they died of a broken heart."[52]

In their journal article about how managers can use the Stockdale Paradox in their work, C.W. Von Bergen and

---

50 Jim Collins, "The Stockdale Paradox," JimCollins.com, accessed February 15, 2021.

51 Ibid

52 Ibid.

Martin Bressler made this argument: "[We have] found with entrepreneurs that too much positive thinking hinders success. Rather, entrepreneurs need to temper their optimism with reality. In business, viewing the world with 'rose colored glasses' can lead to business failure and financial ruin."[53] Positive thinking is good and important, but ignoring a hard reality could hurt us just as much as dwelling on it too much.

The Stockdale Paradox, which combines a stark realism with absolute confidence in a positive outcome, helps us see this tension in our own lives. Endurance and strength don't come from optimism alone. In fact, thinking that our best ideas will immediately revolutionize our lives sets us up for incredible disappointment. Instead, we endure when we combine an unwavering confidence that we will succeed with a willingness to look honestly at reality. Systems cannot save us from delusion. But when we can see the truth, maintain our faith in a positive outcome, look for signs of progress, and keep taking action, we have the right mindset for using systems responsibly.

FACING LIMITATION

As entrepreneurs, we're constantly surrounded by self-help gurus and motivational speakers telling us we can do everything we set our minds to. They say those things for a reason. We have immense creative energy inside of us, and many

---

53 C. W. Von Bergen and Martin S. Bressler, "How Managers Use the Stockdale Paradox to Balance the Now and the Next," *Administrative Issues Journal: Connecting Education, Practice, and Research* 7, no. 2 (winter 2017): 70–80.

opportunities and freedoms in front of us. We can honor that power and take responsibility for our lives.

But we cannot do everything.

As finite beings, we cannot do *most* of the things we wish we could do. Here is a list of pretty great things I already know with 100 percent certainty that I will die having never done:

- Get onto the Forbes 30 Under 30 list
- Marry a high school sweetheart
- Be a professional athlete
- Raise a first-born son
- Become a surgeon
- Introduce my daughter to my Grandpa C
- Look good in a pixie haircut
- Be the valedictorian of my graduating class
- Backpack through Europe in my twenties
- Experience life as an extrovert

The list of things I will *actually* die having never done will be much longer. We need to sit with this for a minute.

Is it possible for us to find joy in the missing out?

Thomas Merton, a mystic in the early twentieth century, wrote about this in a powerful way that changed my entire perspective on our limitations. He said:

> "One who is content with what he has, and who accepts the fact that he inevitably misses very much in life, is far better off than one who has much more but worries about

> all he may be missing...We cannot master everything, taste everything, understand everything, drain every experience to his last dregs. But if we have the courage to let almost everything else go, we will probably be able to retain the one thing necessary for us, whatever it might be... Happiness consists in finding out precisely what the one thing necessary may be in our lives, and then gladly relinquishing all the rest."[54]

This may not sound like an encouraging statement, but imagine the freedom of having your feet firmly on the ground, eyes wide open, as you sink yourself fully into the joy of this exact moment. When you can do that, you can experience deep meaning in the here and now of entrepreneurship.

Accepting your limitations allows you to calibrate your eureka moments to match what you can truly do—what I call "human-sizing" your expectations. From there, you will be in a stronger position to use systems to experience a sense of progress and make your ideas real. Systems require you to make decisions, commit to a path, and act—and these things get much easier when you're willing to close the door on trying to capture everything at once.

I'll never argue that human-sizing our expectations isn't disappointing. It is! Making a list of things I'll never do wasn't enjoyable. Recognizing what we can't do, or what we have to set aside, or what might not be available to us in this season of our lives, is not fun. Real grief can be a part of this process.

---

54 Thomas Merton, *No Man Is an Island* (New York: Houghton Mifflin Harcourt Publishing Company, 1983), 130.

But when we acknowledge and release our disappointment, we will find ourselves getting disappointed far less often. We can be fully present for the things we can do, and experience gratitude for the good things that are here now.

LOOKING FOR PROGRESS ALONG THE WAY

In college, I took a psychology class where we were expected to train rats in the Skinner method of pushing on a lever to get a treat. I was assigned a little white female rat named Charlie. Every day I would go into the lab to train Charlie in the Skinner box. As the weeks went by, I didn't think she was doing very well. She made the same mistakes repeatedly and spent most of her time trying to escape the box. At the end of the semester, I created a graph of Charlie's progress. To my surprise, the graph showed steady, consistent improvement over the course of her training. I couldn't see it in our daily practice, but it was happening all the same.

Entrepreneurs experience this exact same tendency, but with the additional challenge that we regularly move the goalpost without taking the time to celebrate our achievements. What would happen if we took the time to measure metrics that were meaningful to us so we could see the upward trajectory, even during endless projects or "two steps forward, one step back" progress? How would our experience shift if we took the time to celebrate the daily work, the small wins, and the milestones along the way?

When you run a marathon, you want to see those mile markers tick by. Your business is no different, but it's up to you to make the signs and stake them in the ground. Your experience of this journey matters. Progress in a complex system isn't always obvious, so it's worth the work to use simpler systems to give yourself a sense of forward motion.

TAKING IMPERFECT ACTION

Armed with human-sized expectations and a willingness to celebrate your progress, it becomes much easier to put one foot in front of the other. Even when you use systems to maximize your impact, you can still expect to make some messes while you're at it.

One of my favorite coaches for small business owners is named Stephanie Hayes. Stephanie is well versed in the start-up world and has started a successful software company herself, but she works mainly with bootstrapped small business owners. I was curious why she chose to focus on lifestyle businesses and freelancers, so I asked her what she enjoyed the most about that group of people.

"I like their Franken-businesses," she told me. "You've got a leg over here and an arm over there and they piece this thing together from different places. But they tend to get there faster in the end. I like taking the mess and maturing the mess." Stephanie and I talked about the counterintuitive truth that expecting a mess and embracing limitations makes it easier to move forward. We can embrace the experimentation of the whole thing rather than waiting for perfection before we make a move.

"The credit belongs to the man who is actually in the arena; whose face is marred with dust and sweat; who strives valiantly, who errs and may fall again and again, because there is no effort without error or shortcoming."

—THEODORE ROOSEVELT

***

Once we look squarely at the road ahead of us and start moving forward, we will find ourselves on the journey of actual doing. Our castle-in-the-sky ideas will crash-land into the dirt of real life, and we'll get the chance to make them real. We get to participate in the act of creation. The work is meaningful, deep, and very, very messy. The goal for all of us is to learn to thrive right where we are today.

KEY TAKEAWAYS FROM CHAPTER 8:

- Unrealistic expectations will rob you of joy in your business.
- Facing your limitations may be disappointing in the short run but will ultimately free you to make the most of what you are able to do.
- Progress won't announce itself to you; it is important to make the effort to see it.
- The right expectations will enable you to take action.

CONTINUE READING TO LEARN ABOUT TWO ENTREPRENEURIAL REALITIES—THE MESSY MIDDLE AND ITERATIVE PROBLEM-SOLVING—THAT WILL GIVE YOU THE CHANCE TO PRACTICE ALIGNING YOUR EXPECTATIONS.

QUESTIONS FOR REFLECTION AND DISCUSSION:

1. Where have unrealistic expectations made entrepreneurship more difficult for you? What might it look like to human-size those expectations?
2. Where might adjusted expectations make it easier for you to move forward into imperfect action?
3. What practices could you incorporate into your life to help you see the progress you're making?

CHAPTER 9

CORE PRINCIPLE TWO: EMBRACING THE MESSY MIDDLE

"The artist committing himself to his calling has volunteered for hell, whether he knows it or not. He will be dining for the duration on a diet of isolation, rejection, self-doubt, despair, ridicule, contempt, and humiliation."

—STEVEN PRESSFIELD

The journey from eureka moment to Eureka Result is tough. Most entrepreneurs don't just get tired—we also find ourselves getting wounded along the way.

I met Joanna when we were both in the early phases of building our businesses. I was working as an Independent Business Manager, and she had just quit her job to start a coaching program. We had lost touch over the years, but as I prepared to write this book, we connected to talk about our own experiences.

Joanna caught me up on what had been going on since we last talked. "The first year, I was so excited. I felt like I was living my best life—living the dream," she said. "But when I first launched my membership, I wasn't thrilled with my results. And by year two, it started to sink in that this is my life now. I got a part-time job just for the social interaction."

Joanna, like most entrepreneurs, had been inundated with success stories from marketers selling their programs. Webinars and Facebook ads crowed about entrepreneurs who launched their first funnels and made a million dollars immediately (we've already established there's a lot more behind the scenes, but you can't see that in the ads). Joanna dove into the programs and followed the gurus' instructions to the letter, but she experienced trial and error and initial struggles rather than the success she had been promised. The complex system of her business didn't match the overnight success stories she kept hearing. She blamed herself and felt ashamed by what she felt was her failure to achieve those results.

"I kept telling myself this business has to work—it has to work, it has to work," Joanna told me. "It was this hamster wheel mentality that building a successful business would be the key to happiness."

That's when Joanna started to experience a deeper impact on her sense of identity. "I thought I would be a teacher forever," she told me. "So, when I quit teaching, I lost a bit of my identity. I like being productive. I like making things. I like finishing things. I like building things. But when things don't work in my business, I don't get that feeling. And I don't know how to get out of that hole."

I empathized deeply with what Joanna was telling me. I don't miss having a corporate job, but I miss many elements of that environment—things like showing up, knowing what a good job looks like, doing a good job, and getting paid for it. I miss knowing what to do to earn a promotion.

When I started my business, I knew it would push me to grow and learn. But I had no idea how steep that learning curve would be, or how many areas of my brain and identity would be pushed to their extremes. I thrived in corporate and academic settings, but out on my own, there was no cushion between me and my most destructive mindset patterns, my worst habits, and the external factors I had used to bolster my sense of identity. I was building a brand-new complex system, and I was uncomfortable with the uncertainties of that process.

Embracing the inherent messiness of entrepreneurship—what has been coined "the messy middle"—has not come easily to me. When business leader after business leader reminded me that arrival doesn't exist, I didn't want to hear it. When I experienced dips, hit walls, and could only see my progress in hindsight, I kept hoping I would come across my own eureka moment and immediate transformation. It took me a while to see the marathon from eureka moment to Eureka Result as a positive thing.

I'm so grateful for everyone who taught me critical elements of what it means to thrive in the messy middle: recognizing entrepreneurship as a journey in personal development, taking radical personal responsibility, embracing life as a permanent rookie, and waging war against my own resistance.

ENTREPRENEURSHIP AS PERSONAL DEVELOPMENT

"Many business problems are personal problems in disguise."

—MICHAEL PORT

Before I was an entrepreneur, I was a Practice Area Senior Business Analyst. I took my work seriously, but I didn't identify *myself* with that role. Once I started my business, I was surprised to find that calling myself an "entrepreneur" had a much deeper impact on my sense of who I was in the world. It opened up endless options to me and carried extra responsibility with it too.

Any time a life experience impacts our identity, we face risk. Even as we add the positive identity of "entrepreneur," some of our old, safe identities are challenged. We often lose the daily community of other people doing the same work, a boss to give us clear direction and praise, norms that tell us how to behave, and external markers of success like a promotion or a raise. How do we cope when the old pillars of our identity are no longer there?

I remember the exact moment I heard it. I was driving down Main Street and listening to Amy Porterfield's podcast *Online Marketing Made Easy.* Amy was interviewing an expert in habit formation named James Clear, and his perspective on how humans change their behavior immediately caught my attention.

"Every action you take is a vote for the type of person you want to become," James said.[55] I stopped daydreaming and turned up the volume. He continued, "We all have a collection of identities, and we also have beliefs that are part of our identity. Sometimes those beliefs build us up, like 'I'm the type of person who finishes what I set out to do,' but sometimes those beliefs hold us back, like 'I'm terrible at remembering names,'... or 'I have a sweet tooth.'"[56]

James went on to explain that behavior changes and our beliefs are a two-way street: "the things you believe can influence the way you act, and the way you act can influence the things you believe."[57] James argued that while working on our mindset is valuable, a more effective route is to shift the trajectory of our behavior and see each individual action as a step toward becoming the type of person we want to be. Over time, those actions will become habits, and those habits will become a part of our identity. When James talked about the "trajectory of our behavior," he was referring to systems. He has even gone as far to say elsewhere ,"You do not rise to the level of your goals. You fall to the level of your systems."[58]

---

55 James Clear, "How to Create Atomic Habits with James Clear," December 26, 2019, episode 295, in *Online Marketing Made Easy*, produced by Amy Porterfield, podcast, MP3 audio.

56 Ibid.

57 Ibid.

58 James Clear, "3-2-1: On Systems vs. Goals, Identity-Based Habits, and the Lessons of Life," JamesClear.com, January 2, 2020.

While James was talking, I couldn't stop thinking about what this has meant for my own business. Looking back, I realize I'm not the same person I was when I started the business. When I was in college, I decided I wasn't cut out for two things: sales and leadership. I was good at getting things done, but I didn't want to be in the spotlight. Years later, I started my business with the knowledge that sales and leadership would be core elements of my work, but I was apprehensive about both things. Now, after thousands of daily votes for the type of person I wanted to be, I'm a leader in a way I never was before. I'm more confident and better at setting boundaries and protecting my time. People have begun to call me a visionary. While I was busy building my business, deep shifts outside of my conscious awareness. Entrepreneurship has become one of the most powerful tools for personal change in my life.

My guess is that if you look back at who you were when you started your business, you'll see the same identity-level shifts in how you're showing up every day. Like I discovered training Charlie the rat, we often make progress we can't see until we stop long enough to look back. We *are* entrepreneurs because we've been doing the work—it's part of who we are. The systems we use to take daily action aren't just helping us move forward; they are changing us at a profound level.

> *"Entrepreneurship is the greatest self-development program ever created."*
>
> —JOHN JANTSCH

Starting a business requires us to give up some of the normal identity pillars that came with our job before. When we take risks in leadership, we will fail at times, and if our sense of worth is tied to our work, our identity may rise and fall with our business. We have to be careful to recognize our worth as people is independent of what happens in our businesses. When we embrace the idea that every step, including our failures, takes us further on a trajectory toward deep growth, we can find meaning and fulfillment in the messy middle.

As we embrace the growth that comes with this journey, we can take another step: taking responsibility for our own lives.

RADICAL PERSONAL RESPONSIBILITY

"If you could kick the person in the pants responsible for most of your trouble, you wouldn't sit for a month."

—THEODORE ROOSEVELT

Ash Ambirge is an incredible example of seeing entrepreneurship as personal development and taking radical responsibility for her own life. Ash currently leads a seven-figure powerhouse business, but as she shares in her book, *The Middle Finger Project,* she spent most of her early years dreaming of a traditional middle-class lifestyle. For her, the perfect life looked like "vinyl siding and carpeted staircases and two-car garages and freshly cut bagels."[59]

59 Ash Ambirge, *The Middle Finger Project: Trash Your Imposter Syndrome and Live the Unf*ckwithable Life You Deserve* (New York: Portfolio, 2020), 72.

Ash was determined to follow all the rules to achieve her dream. She was thrust into independence as a young woman after her mom passed away, making her all the more desperate to get everything right so she could provide for herself. As a talented marketer, Ash rocketed up the ranks in her first corporate job, which ultimately granted her the lifestyle she imagined. Ash wasn't happy, though, and she began to explore what it would look like to be paid as a writer. She even quit her job to start her own business, but after a series of rejections and mistakes, she got another job.[60]

A regular blog routine kept Ash's writing dream alive for years, but she felt trapped and unwilling to break "the rules." One night, everything came to a head when she walked out of her abusive boyfriend's life. She stepped into her car, put on her seatbelt, and realized she had nowhere to go. Ash drove to a Kmart parking lot and spent the night in her car. She realized she would need to rebuild her life on her own.

Inspired by the voice of a radio DJ announcing a project that was available for preorder, Ash put together a description and a buy button offering her services as a writer. She sent an email to her blog subscribers and waited. Within hours, Ash had made her first $2,000. She never went back to her old life.

Looking back, Ash says, "I am grateful for that hardship that night in the Kmart parking lot because it forced me to follow

---

60 Ash Ambirge, "The 67 Emotions of Unconventional Success: My Story," *The Middle Finger Project* (blog), December 3, 2010.

a dangerous idea without getting in my own way...I simply got started because I had to."[61]

Ash shares her story so openly because she wants more people to understand what can happen when they throw out the rulebook and trust their ideas. "Get out there and make something disobedient," she commands us. "Be anything but normal. Create. Contribute. Take risks...Create your own version of success...And, as always, never stop following your most dangerous ideas."[62] Ash believes in self-reliance rather than looking to others to have the answers for us. We have the opportunity to create, lead, build, and take up space. Entrepreneurship isn't the only way we can do that, but it is one of the most powerful choices.

Most of us weren't raised to take this level of responsibility over our lives. We learn obedience from our parents and school environments and can find ourselves accepting jobs that keep us on the trajectory of following orders rather than building our own lives. When we step outside of those narratives, the world opens up. We can lead, create, and make free choices. We can build our own systems. When we're in the arena and nothing is guaranteed, freedom can be frightening, but taking ownership over our lives can help us thrive in the midst of uncertainty.

---

61 Ash Ambirge, *The Middle Finger Project: Trash Your Imposter Syndrome and Live the Unf*ckwithable Life You Deserve*, 138.

62 Ash Ambirge, *The Middle Finger Project: Trash Your Imposter Syndrome and Live the Unf*ckwithable Life You Deserve*, 276.

Stepping into this level of ownership as an entrepreneur means something else too—we will always be new at something. Always.

BEING A PROFESSIONAL ROOKIE

I had just finished a presentation about my business for Georgetown's Startup Showcase when a man walked up to me. He looked familiar, but I couldn't place him. "I'd like to help you however I can," he said, and handed me his business card. His name was Tom Raffa.

I looked up Tom's name and discovered that over three decades, Tom had built the largest B-certified accounting firm in the world. It employed over 250 people and was built on a unique and powerful culture of recognizing business as a force for good. Tom is a pioneer of social entrepreneurship, and he quickly became one of my heroes. His story brings me back to earth every time I think I should have this entrepreneurship thing perfected by now.

Tom began his career as a CPA within a large consulting firm but left in 1984 to strike out on his own. He was disappointed by companies that were filled with good people but still focused only on the bottom line. "I didn't want to just build the best CPA firm in the world," he told me. "I wanted to build the best firm *for* the world." From day one, Raffa had a deep and unique mission.

I asked Tom what it looked like to build his team, and he opened up about how challenging it was in the early years. His first employee joined just to keep busy while she looked for another job, but she ended up staying with the company. Eight months later, Tom hired their next team member. He told me, "My strategy was to hire someone billable when everyone was at 130 percent, which worked okay until someone quit. Then it felt like a huge step back and wreaked havoc until we could find someone new." Tom began to train up leaders within the team, but he initially protected them too much from the consequences of their own choices. Tom realized that separating them from the impacts of failure actually weakened their ability to innovate and lead. Like every rookie, Tom learned as he grew. Tom began to step back and allow his team to experience the ups and downs of entrepreneurship while he walked the walk in his own life. Any time Tom mastered a role, he would hire someone else to do it and then move on to something new.

Tom told me he saw entrepreneurship as a smart form of gambling, so the iterations of learning to lead didn't surprise him. "I saw myself as a scientist," he said. "I wouldn't do anything that would blow up the lab, but I wasn't surprised by failure. If things didn't work, I would mix up the ingredients and try again." Tom recognized the power of the systems under the work he did, and he strategically noticed and tweaked them to make his business stronger.

Tom also knew his journey with the company would place him permanently on the cutting edge of his own abilities. He was always doing something that was completely new to him. "When I had a fifty-person company, it was the first time I had a fifty-person company," he told me. "Then when I had a fifty-one-person company, it was the first time I had a fifty-one-person company." Over thirty years, Tom's vision never changed. He knew life was too short to build a business for a small reason. Because of his clear mission and his willingness to be a permanent rookie in his own business, he built a legacy that has impacted thousands of lives.

Tom showed me what it looked like to live a meaningful life as an entrepreneur. He didn't fall victim to the temptation to make everything an existential threat—he understood he had the chance to play the game and take risks, and he was able to carry that with a sense of lightness that is hard to find in the entrepreneurial community. By choosing entrepreneurship, we've signed up for a career's worth of first times and the chance to grow on a much deeper level as a result. That's a gift we shouldn't take for granted.

Entrepreneurship is an interesting paradox. On the one hand, we can recognize the deep power of our work for ourselves and the world; on the other, we can hold everything loosely because we recognize our work doesn't define our value and failure is an integral part of the process. Holding these things in tension gives us the spine and resilience we need to go to battle against our greatest nemesis: resistance.

WAGING A WAR AGAINST RESISTANCE

"Rule of thumb: The more important a call or action is to our soul's evolution, the more Resistance we will feel toward pursuing it."

—STEVEN PRESSFIELD

Thomas Aronica started his payments business, PCI Professionals, in 2008. After years of serving his clients individually, Thomas began to notice a theme in their frustrations about the software tools available to them. "Everyone was coming to us asking for something, anything, that would make their bookkeeping software and invoicing and payment systems talk to each other," he told me. One evening in 2017, Thomas was having dinner with a friend who was venting to him about how hard it was to get paid consistently by the tenants in his rental properties. He told Thomas he wished something existed that would streamline the process and make his life easier. That night, Thomas couldn't sleep—his mind wouldn't shut off. As he stepped out of the shower the next morning, his eureka moment hit him—he could create that product to help his clients. The next day, he posted a job ad seeking a software developer to turn that dream into reality.

The process of development took a year, and Thomas launched the product in late 2018. "Within two weeks, we knew we had something big on our hands," he told me. "Social influencers and financial institutions were reaching out to us right away when they got wind of what we were doing."

Thomas's story is a great example of how it takes ten years to be an overnight success. He was so tuned into his market that he was able to solve their biggest problem and immediately make a huge splash. But even then—in the middle of the best-case scenario—resistance in his own mind began to make itself known.

As more people came flooding in to use the software, it quickly became clear that the software they had created just to help their clients was taking on a life of its own and would need to be split into a separate business. When I asked Thomas about the most challenging aspects of his entrepreneurial journey, he mentioned that shift as one of the most difficult seasons of his twelve-year journey. He told me, "We had been invested in the payments business for so long that we thought like payments people. We had been doing it the same way forever."

Thomas felt the resistance of having to shift his own focus, both as a leader and with the culture of his team, while simultaneously building a completely different type of business than the one he had before. Embracing the opportunity required a hectic journey of raising funds, experimenting with distribution channels, expanding the team from five to twenty-five people, and investing in a leadership team before they were able to relaunch Biller Genie as a fully standalone business by the beginning of 2020. Every step of the process was completely new to Thomas, and he felt his "permanent rookie" status acutely. But it was worth the push, and Biller Genie was perfectly positioned for another wave of growth as businesses were forced to move to online bill payment and invoicing during a global pandemic.

"The hardest thing has been to go from doer to strategic leader," Thomas told me about that time. "I had never worked for anybody but myself because I started my first business right out of college. I had never seen how large-scale businesses do this." Thomas leaned into the resistance and sought out great mentors, and he has made huge strides in his business as he continues to adapt and grow.

If you've ever skipped the same project on your to-do list for months on end, or stalled out right before finishing a task, or procrastinated endlessly on something important to you, then you're familiar with resistance. We all experience it.

Resistance is inside your own head. It's the voice telling you that being a professional rookie isn't safe. It's that sinking feeling you get when you crest one hill only to see five more in front of you. It's that nudge that lands you in the middle of a YouTube video when you're supposed to be writing your book. When you're running the marathon from eureka idea to Eureka Result, your brain will continually insist that the energy you have at your disposal isn't enough to get you across the finish line. So why even try?

The good news is that you can strengthen your will and weaken the power of resistance in your mind by noticing it, honoring it as a signal, and verbalizing what it's telling you. As Dr. Robert Wicks notes in his article on resistance, "two ways we can improve our own self-awareness are by increasing our sensitivity to our defensiveness, and by taking what actions we can to outflank our resistance."[63]

Ask yourself—what is your brain trying to dodge or protect you from? You might come up with answers like:

- "I'm not moving this project forward because I'm not sure what to do next and my brain is moving me toward things that are clearer."

---

63 Robert Wicks, "Outflank Your Own Resistances to Change," *Psychology Today*, September 14, 2009.

- "I'm procrastinating because I am afraid that if I post this, I'll get rejected."
- "I'm cleaning out my inbox instead of doing strategic planning because I've decided that I'm not good at strategic planning, and it will be hard."

Once you know why your brain is trying to protect you, you can decide whether or not to listen to it. You can clarify what's unclear, make decisions, process your fear, question your assumptions, and use systems to move forward. As an entrepreneur, you no longer have a boss to force you to do things you don't want to do; it's up to you to keep showing up to do the work.

***

The journey of entrepreneurship isn't easy. It can wound us, change us, and leave us in the messy middle far longer than we might like. But when we see the process as something that helps us grow, take responsibility for who we are in the midst of it, choose to become a professional rookie, and lean into resistance, we can build the muscles we need to thrive in the messy middle.

KEY TAKEAWAYS FROM CHAPTER 9:

- You're becoming a different person in this journey, and your trajectory is more important than your position.
- Radical personal responsibility will help you take a leadership role in your own life.
- Be prepared to always be a rookie.

- Acknowledging and leaning into resistance will weaken its power.
- When you learn how to thrive in the messy middle, you'll be more equipped to leverage systems to persevere on the road toward turning your best ideas into reality.

CONTINUE READING TO LEARN HOW THE ROAD TO EUREKA RESULTS IS AN ENDLESS JOURNEY OF ITERATIVE PROBLEM-SOLVING.

QUESTIONS FOR REFLECTION AND DISCUSSION:

1. How comfortable are you in the messy middle of your business?
2. How often do you notice resistance in your work? What triggers it the most?
3. Are there areas in your life and business where you have abdicated your personal responsibility? How can you step back into a leadership role in those areas?

CHAPTER 10

CORE PRINCIPLE THREE: ITERATIVE PROBLEM-SOLVING

"Entrepreneurship is, by definition, about experimenting—trying something, seeing what the results are, learning from the results, and then trying it again."

—CANDIDA BRUSH

Once you have a mental baseline of strong, honest expectations and a willingness to learn how to thrive in the messy middle, what does progress actually look like? How do people operate within these complex systems and achieve a Eureka Result?

I've started collecting the different terms people use to describe their experience of growing a business:

- An upward spiral
- "The swirl"
- A roller coaster
- An endless experiment
- The messy middle
- A game
- Endless problem-solving

In conversations with dozens of entrepreneurs, I never once heard a story where everything fell together effortlessly; instead, I was inspired by story after story of growth and resilience. Every entrepreneur I've met has an experience of iterative problem-solving, which means an ongoing sequence of tweaks, improvements, and new problems to solve inside their systems. Most people described this process as messy, frustrating, *and* deeply meaningful; building stamina for these cycles is a huge part of what it means to thrive as an entrepreneur. Three ways to build that stamina are embracing experimentation, picking which problems we would like to solve, and anticipating failure.

EMBRACING THE EXPERIMENT

Perfectionism is a common roadblock for many entrepreneurs. Advice about lowering our standards or focusing on getting things done is common, but the most unique perspective I've ever heard came from my interview with Ash Ambirge during her launch for *The Middle Finger Project.* When I asked Ash about how she combats perfectionism, she said, "Perfectionism is useful for keeping you to standards, but the other side that has to balance that out is saying, 'Guess what? It will never really be done.'"

Ash shared about how she had toiled over many projects until she thought she had finally arrived, only to come back the next week to tweak something else. It brought her to the conclusion she shared with me: "The other side of perfectionism is the acceptance of reality; you're going to be iterating no matter what, so it's a fool's errand to keep going on this quest to make it the best thing it could possibly be. But it *will* get better, so shoot for better instead of best."

I loved the idea of recognizing the endless iteration of my work, but an ongoing challenge for me has been to detach myself from my work. It's natural for me to look at my revenue and see my own value through those things. When my business is going well, I feel like a solid entrepreneur. When something goes wrong, I gravitate toward, "I'm bad at this," when a more useful way of thinking is, "Well, that didn't work out very well. How can I tweak my system to get a better result next time?"

When we build something of our own, our business becomes deeply connected to our identity. Living like a scientist running a lab can help us create a healthy level of distance. We have hypotheses, we're running experiments, and we're iterating our systems based on the results. Every scientist could tell you that a result that disproves a hypothesis is actually a successful experiment rather than a failure. Anytime we live inside a complex system, this approach is critical.

Thomas Edison invented the lightbulb after over one thousand different attempts. I imagine him, sitting down on a leather armchair across from a journalist with a notepad. On the table between them is a glowing lightbulb. Thomas says,

"I tried over one thousand different combinations before discovering this one."

The journalist's eyebrows go up. He writes "one thousand failed experiments" on his notepad. He looks up and asks, "How did it feel to fail one thousand times?"[64]

Thomas pauses. He looks down at the lightbulb on the table, thinking about what electric light will mean for his world and for future generations. With a slight smile, he responds, "I didn't fail one thousand times. The lightbulb was an invention with one thousand steps."[65]

EXPERIMENTS IN BOLDNESS

Shelly Davies is one of the most incredible examples of embracing experimentation I have ever met. Shelly is a plain language coach and incredible expert in her field. Not only is she brilliant at coaching corporations and professionals to leave behind corporate jargon, but she does her work in an incredibly unique way. Shelly has a significant tattoo connecting her to her Māori heritage on her chin and short, pink hair. When Shelly walks into a corporate setting to do a training, people remember her and her brand. When I spoke with Shelly, I wanted to understand what had given her the courage to build such a powerful and memorable business.

---

64 Ram Kumar, "The Greatest Inventor 'Thomas Alva Edison's' Vision on Failures," *Medium*, December 29, 2019.

65 Ibid.

In her calm, assured way, Shelly told me, "Quite possibly the most powerful tool in my entire business journey of growth is always pausing and looking for evidence. Because if we don't lock that evidence in, and if we don't search for it, recognize it, grab on to it, then we have to keep relearning things; we continually find ourselves in a place where we're doubting ourselves again, or wondering, 'Should I do it this way?'"

Shelly listens to her intuition but uses objective evidence to test out an idea before committing to it. She gave me an amazing example of how this happened in the early stages of her business when she said:

"If my gut says, Shelly, you should use language on your website, I think it through. And I always do. I'll do some catastrophizing and ask, what's the worst thing that could happen? The worst that could happen is that someone gets upset—can I live with that? Yes. Is it worth testing it out to see if there are any benefits? Yes. Okay, then I'm going to try it. Then after I've done it, at some point I'll look back and think, 'What has happened since I first used that word on LinkedIn, or on my website, or whatever?' And there is usually a list of good outcomes. So, I keep doing it."

Shelly makes a regular habit of implementing a new system, looking at the data, and adjusting accordingly. When I asked her later about building her confidence to take risks, she brought me back to experimentation. She told me she would take a risk with the full expectation that it might not work. "If it didn't work, it didn't feel like a failure because I was just testing it out," she told me. "So, I seek the evidence of whether or not it's worked. And if it hasn't, I don't do it again, but if it has, I do it more."

Shelly's system of experimentation has given her incredible strength and resiliency. What would it look like for us to follow her lead?

> *"All life is an experiment. The more experiments you make the better."*
>
> —RALPH WALDO EMERSON

TACKLING CHALLENGES AS THEY COME

Another story that demonstrates continuous growth through experimentation comes from my aunt—Cindy Gasior. Today, Cindy is a celebrated home stager in Tulsa, Oklahoma. Fifteen years ago, she was an accountant who ran her own firm alongside a thriving rental property business. The transition between the two has been quite the journey.

Cindy always had a knack for building beautiful homes. When she found herself longing for more creative work, she enrolled in a class on interior design and landed an internship with a local designer. She ultimately shut down her accounting firm to start her own home staging business. The experiment had begun.

Over the past fifteen years, Cindy has cleared hurdles over and over again. When her workload became too heavy, her husband took over the rental property business so she could focus. When she found it difficult to break into the clique of her local real estate market, she moved her business to a larger city. When her furniture was destroyed in rental storage units, she rented her first warehouse space. Each step simultaneously enabled her business to grow further and opened the door to a new set of challenges.

Cindy has built an impressive business, but that doesn't mean the challenges have stopped coming or she's figured it all out. Each summit has revealed a new mountain to climb. As long as her business exists, Cindy will continue to iterate and evolve. Her story was a helpful reminder to me that every business involves an endless process of experimentation, tackling one problem at a time, and learning. Most of us are tempted to stop moving forward until we figure it all out, but forward motion is the only way we can gain the knowledge experimentation provides.

The good news? As entrepreneurs, even though we will never achieve a problem-free business, we get to choose what problems we actually want to solve. That is the next principle of iterative problem-solving.

PICKING YOUR PROBLEMS

As I spoke with more and more entrepreneurs, I began to hear a common theme that doesn't quite make it into the marketing materials of all the courses we buy: entrepreneurship is a complex system built for solving problems, and you'll never stop doing it. You have the amazing power to decide which problems you most enjoy solving—and this is a gift—but you don't get to decide whether or not you have them. It can be a long process of discovery to find that sweet spot, and then a journey of discipline to stay in it.

Here are three of my favorite stories:

Ivan Mladenovic is a talented teacher, motivator, and salesman. When Ivan started a retail IT support company in 2009, he envisioned building a large company and selling it. But Ivan quickly learned that consumer services like IT support didn't often become a big saleable asset without franchising. He didn't want to deal with managing a large group of different business owners and franchises across the country because that wasn't a set of problems that excited him.

Instead, Ivan decided to see his business as a tool for consistent cash flow, nudging him to pivot to a recurring subscription model for his clients. Today, Ivan's problems to solve include building a structured mid-level management team for his company, deciding how to best invest their cash to grow, and finding an integrator who knows his business to partner with him. "I know that each growth step means I'll need to take a hit so I can build the engine to get to the next level," he told me. "We're always cycling up and down, but these are great problems to solve."

Rachel Mazza began her business as a freelance content writer with dreams of building an empire. She was a successful marketer and ended up swamped with work, so, like Ivan, she hired a team and began to build an agency. Her team specialized in conversion content, and they had no problem finding new clients, but Rachel experienced problem after problem behind the scenes. She had to learn how to train junior copywriters, deal with a group of clients she liked less and less, and juggle everything without efficient systems.

Over time, Rachel learned exactly what it would take to overhaul her agency and rebuild it into something amazing, but there was one problem: she was burnt out and didn't want to solve these problems anymore. So, Rachel shut down her agency and returned to freelancing. Rachel has spent the past several years providing high-ticket specialty services, which has given her the lifestyle she always wanted. Today, Rachel's problems include up-leveling from copywriting to consulting and balancing client work with her ongoing marketing priorities. Rachel has the courage and the power to adapt her business to match her skills, her lifestyle, and the problems she wants to solve.

Dean Edelson, a successful premium freelance copywriter, told me he'd tried to build a team at one point, but he didn't enjoy it. It took him more time to train someone else than to do it himself, and it wasn't worth the effort. Now, as a solopreneur, he commands a high price for his work, has the lifestyle he wants, and doesn't let greed or a need for validation sour his mindset.

Dean's business looks exactly like he wants it to look today, and he is content with that. Dean told me, "you have to decide what problems you want to solve. Someone out there is making eight figures, somebody else is making a billion dollars, and it's simply a different set of problems. You have to step back and say, 'I'd be happy fixing these types of challenges,' and build your business around that."

"The true entrepreneur knows he'll keep trying forever."

—MAXIME LAGACÉ

Every business model has pros and cons. As you think through which problems you'd most like to solve, it's worth looking honestly at your options so you don't run into that wall of unmet expectations we've talked about. Here are a few of the major perks and problems to keep in mind:

- **Agency** (you have a team of people assisting you in delivering a service to your clients):
  - Problems: your team doing bad work, your team doing no work, needing to train, needing to hire and fire, others relying on you for their livelihoods
  - Perks: leaving for a month and coming back to find your business humming along, focusing on your zone of genius while others focus on theirs, community, deeper impact, creating jobs for other people
- **Physical Retail or eCommerce** (selling products in person or online):
  - Problems: constant marketing, supply chain challenges, customer service/refund requests, expensive shipping and overhead costs, big industry companies can steal your idea and crush you
  - Perks: easier to delegate, short transaction cycle (they buy it, you ship it), attractive for outside funding, can scale fast and sell, easier for product to get better and cheaper as you grow
- **Information Products** (selling courses, e-books, and other products that teach):

  - Problems: students asking you questions all the time, a huge up-front workload, having to get a ton of new customers, low completion rates, more customers = more angry people in your life
  - Perks: nearly infinite scalability, up-front work pays off for a long time, building authority as an expert, can be easy to maintain once you're up and running, lots of opportunity for deep, creative work
- **Freelancing/solo service provider** (providing a service directly):
  - Problems: if you get sick, revenue goes to zero, you're doing the same type of work repeatedly and might get sick of it, your own hang ups are the main reason for every problem in your business, isolation, your growth is capped by your capacity, service quality can go down if you grow too much/too fast
  - Perks: everything's done exactly as you like it, no one else is relying on you for their income, pivoting is easy, you make the rules (ideally), you have a discrete number of happy clients

"You have to love the game you're playing, because you'll never stop playing it."

—SHAWN TWING

ANTICIPATING FAILURE

I watched Brené Brown's Netflix special when it first came out, and there were many pieces that spoke to me. But there was one piece in particular that floored me, and it was this quote: "If you're brave with your life, if you choose to live in the arena, you are going to get your ass kicked. You are going to fail. You are going to know heartbreak."[66] Brené went on to talk about leaders who would declare they were willing to risk failure in their lives, probably expecting Brené to pat them on the back for their courage. Instead, she would stop them short. "No, you don't hear me...somewhere in there you missed it," she'd say. "It's not that you're going to *risk* failure. *You are going to fail if you're brave with your life.*"[67]

I've always liked the idea of risking failure as an entrepreneur. I don't know how I feel about guaranteeing it. But any scientist will tell you—if you run experiments that always give you the result you want, you're running weak experiments that will do nothing for you. As you build your business, if you never screw up, you're in trouble. You can't grow unless you stretch, and when you stretch, you sometimes fail. Like Shelly Davies shared with me, failure is simply a signal that we need to tweak some things and try again.

Entrepreneurship is an exercise in embracing this kind of failure. If we just look at the success stories, we might miss the sequences of failures those same people walked through:

- Evan Williams, the co-founder of Twitter, created a podcast app and launched it right before Apple added podcasts to iTunes. His company closed shortly thereafter[68]

---

66 Brené Brown, *Call to Courage,* film, directed by Sandra Restrepo, (Los Gatos: Netflix, 2019), streaming, 16:41.

67 Ibid.

68 Annie Pilon, "21 Entrepreneurs Who Failed Big Before Becoming a Success," *Small Business Trends,* last updated November 2, 2017.

- Sir James Dyson, who invented the bagless vacuum, created over five thousand failed prototypes before finding one that worked[69]
- Vera Wang tried unsuccessfully to skate with the US Olympic figure skating team and was turned down for a promotion at Vogue before setting out on her own[70]
- Milton Hershey created three candy companies, all of which failed, before founding the Hershey Company[71]
- Arianna Huffington's second book was rejected by thirty-six publishers[72]
- Michael Jordan tracked his failures, summarizing them in this famous quote: "I've missed more than nine thousand shots in my career. I've lost almost three hundred games. Twenty-six times, I've been trusted to take the game-winning shot and missed. I've failed over and over and over again in my life. And that is why I succeed."[73]

Raising a daughter has helped to solidify this fact for me more and more. Averee "fails" boldly and without apology all the time. As I write this, she is learning to speak. Most of her words are unintelligible gibberish. But she keeps doing it, and I can hear her words take shape piece by piece. What would it look like for us to publish our best creative work, even when our best feels like it's still in the "unintelligible gibberish" phase? What would happen in our lives and businesses if

69 Ibid.

70 Ibid.

71 Ibid.

72 Ibid.

73 Paul Kasabian, "Michael Jordan's Worst Career Game Stats, Shooting Performances and Misses," *Bleacher Report*, May 10, 2020.

we embraced the experiment of it all, stepped into our roles as perpetual rookies, and did our learning and our work in public?

***

Before we can truly leverage the power of systems, this is the approach we need to take. Systems provide shape to our experiments, help us understand our progress, and give us resources as we walk through the messy middle between eureka moment and Eureka Result. With that in mind, let's dive into the five specific core systems that will strengthen your business.

KEY TAKEAWAYS FROM CHAPTER 10:

- Entrepreneurship is an ongoing journey of iterative problem-solving.
- Seeing our business as an experiment can give us strength and resiliency in our businesses.
- We never stop solving problems in our business, but we have a lot of power to determine which problems we want to solve.
- Failure is inevitable and important.

CONTINUE READING TO LEARN ABOUT THE FIVE CORE SYSTEMS TO HELP YOU TURN YOUR BEST IDEAS INTO REALITY.

QUESTIONS FOR REFLECTION AND DISCUSSION:

1. Do you ever find yourself expecting your problems to disappear once you arrive at a certain milestone or achieve

a goal? How does it feel to recognize you will have new problems at that perceived pinnacle?

2. What would it look like for you to embrace experimentation and failure more often in your business?
3. What are the problems you want to solve?

PART THREE

CORE SYSTEMS OF EUREKA RESULTS

CHAPTER 11

CORE SYSTEM ONE: RUN THE RIGHT RACE

"If you are working on something really exciting that you really care about, you don't have to be pushed. The vision pulls you."

—STEVE JOBS

A wealthy businessman once went on vacation to a small village on the coast of Mexico.[74] While he was walking on the beach, he saw a small boat dock nearby with a single fisherman inside. Curious, he walked up to the man and saw several large yellowfin tunas on the floor of the boat. The businessman knew the value of these fish and complemented the fisherman on his catch.

74 Courtney Carver, "The Story of the Mexican Fisherman," *The Simplicity Space* (blog), accessed February 18, 2021.

"How long did it take you to catch these fish?" the businessman asked.

The fisherman smiled and replied, "Every morning, I go out in my boat for thirty minutes to fish. I'm the best fisherman in the village."

The businessman's phone vibrated. He looked at the notification to see a panicked text from a team member. His blood pressure rose, but he shoved the phone back into his pocket and turned back to the fisherman. He asked, "If you're the best, why wouldn't you want to stay out longer to catch more fish? How do you spend the rest of your day?"

The fisherman laughed and said, "I love to sleep late, and after I fish, I spend time with my children and my wife, and in the evenings, we walk into the village to drink wine and play guitar with our friends. I have a full and happy life."

The businessman was filled with pity for the naive fisherman. He responded, "I've been around the block a few times, and I know how to see a great business opportunity. You ought to let me help you become more successful. You're missing out on a big thing here. All you have to do is fish more, and that money could buy you a bigger boat. You could build up a full fleet with many fishermen and move to the city to oversee everything."

The fisherman's eyebrows rose. He asked, "How long would that take?"

"Oh, fifteen to twenty years," the businessman replied.

"What would happen after that?" asked the fisherman.

The businessman's eyes lit up. "That's the best part," he said. "Then you can take your company public and make millions!"

The fisherman pursed his lips and paused. "Okay..." he replied. "Then what?"

The businessman said, "After that, you could retire. You could move to a beautiful little village on the coast—sleep late, fish a little, play with your kids, spend time with your wife. What an amazing life, eh? In the evenings, you could even drink wine and play guitar with your friends."[75]

****

It can be easy for us to keep our heads down and keep pushing on the race from eureka idea to Eureka Result. If we can grow, we should. If a door opens, we go through it. But all the efficiency in the world won't get us to the right place if we're on the wrong road to begin with. That's what our friend the businessman failed to understand.

In the summer of 2017, I was working in a large consulting firm I had joined in 2015. I had six months of my MBA program left and was trying to figure out what to do next. I wasn't happy in my job, and none of the jobs appearing on Georgetown's job board appealed to me at all. I was newly married, staring down the barrel of $70K in student debt, and dreaming of building a family and being as present for my

75 Ibid.

children as my mom was for me. My husband was on board with me running a three-month experiment to see if I could make it as a freelancer. I quit my job, applied for a business license, and built my first website on Wix. I styled myself as an "Independent Business Manager" and found my first three clients on Facebook.

I soon discovered a strange cultural gap between the start-up community and the freelance community. My start-up friends were on a mission—building product-based businesses they intended to grow rapidly and sell. "Scale" was the vision, and the energy in a room full of start-up founders was contagious. In contrast, my first clients had a different vision. One had spent a few weeks sleeping in her car in the early phases of building her copywriting business because she wanted freedom and was done with the corporate world. Another quit her lucrative communications career when her daughter was born with a hole in her heart. A third had built a successful SaaS business but had a passion for coaching entrepreneurs. For each of them, freedom was priority number one.

I saw so much good in the start-up space, but with freelancers, I had found my people. A whole new world opened up to me of lifestyle-driven businesses, built on rebellion against corporate norms and driven by a belief that we could design a lifestyle we want. Freelancing brought its own challenges, and I quickly found that achieving that fabled "four-hour work week" was easier said than done.[76] But the more entre-

---

76 Tim Ferriss, *The Four-Hour Work Week* (New York: Harmony Books, 2009).

preneurs I met, the more I learned that the "9 to 5 until you're 65" narrative is only one of many ways to build a life.

Success can be achieved in many different ways, and there are many different types of successful businesses. Before we can build the systems we'll use to run our businesses, we need to make sure the business we're building is the one we actually want. Our first core system, then, is meant to both pinpoint and keep our eyes fixed on what that looks like for us.

The next five chapters are meant to be a field guide for you. We'll build the scaffolding of the core systems you need to make your best ideas real. Contemplating what you want is important, but when you leverage the power of systems to integrate your priorities into the structures that make your life happen, that's where things really begin to change.

PROTECTING YOUR PRIORITIES

> *"We're looking for managing the three dials of abundant time, and daily joy, and financial peace. Those are the three kind of lifestyle elements that you look to manage. And so I've always been attracted to freedom as the highest one, time freedom. [It] brings me joy to have that."*[77]
>
> —DEAN JACKSON

Laura Gale is an incredible example of staying true to her priorities. Her business gives her the life she wants, and

---

77 Dean Jackson, "Life Behind the Scenes with Dean Jackson and James Schramko - Part 6 of 25 - Time Secrets," December 5, 2019, in *SuperFast Business*, produced by James Schramko, podcast, MP3 audio.

she has consciously chosen to ignore the "you're growing or you're dying" rhetoric of so many entrepreneurial gurus. Laura works five hours a day, spends time with her partner, plays with her puppy, and replenishes her creative energy in nature so she can focus her best work on her clients. "It's hard to focus because you get so much advice saying, 'You should be doing this or you should be doing that; you have to scale, you have to hire,'" she told me. "I'm constantly having to draw this boundary that what I want is what Dean Jackson talks about—time freedom, financial peace, and daily joy."

Laura's focused effort didn't happen overnight. She had her own journey of iterations after she left her last corporate job, including stints as a nutrition coach, freelance copywriter, and in-house copywriter before she decided to plant her flag as a ghostwriter. Through years of projects and experiments, Laura learned who she most enjoyed working with and what she wanted to do. Her ability to create deep, high-quality work drew her into a space where she could write entire books in partnership with entrepreneurs she enjoyed.

Laura now works on only three or four high-ticket projects each year, and it's the perfect fit for her. She said, "I'm good at writing books. That's all I want to do. I don't want to build courses. I don't want to build a funnel or do tons of marketing. I just want to write books for people who I enjoy working with."

When Laura sits down to make plans for her business, she asks specific questions in all three areas:

- Financial peace: What does this look like to me? How much money do I want to save each month? How much do I want in retirement savings? Do I want to buy a specific type of home? What dollar amount do I want to set aside to care for my parents?
- Time freedom: Do I define ultimate time freedom as ceasing to work altogether? If not, what do I want to work on? How can I avoid being ruled by what I have to deliver?
- Daily joy: What does my ideal day look like? What can make me feel joyful on a daily basis? What are the small daily habits that improve the quality of my life?

After making her plan, Laura actively sets boundaries and pursues contentment in her own mind. "It releases you from the ongoing pressure to have and do more and more and more," she told me.

Our current entrepreneurship space doesn't celebrate this enough, and being surrounded by a relentless hustle culture can leave us feeling a little rootless. Laura pointed this out too. "It's not a very well-defined space," she said, "so you really have to have quiet time to develop self-awareness and emotional fluency. You have to strip off all the stuff you've accumulated."

Laura actively pursues meditation and periodic therapy so she can build resilience for the long road of entrepreneurship. She sees that "all business problems are people problems." As valuable as systems are, our businesses are living things connected to people, and we are on a constant journey of iteration. Taking the time to ask the question, "What do I truly want this business to do for me?" can help us all stay true to a vision that matches who we are as people.

****

As you read Laura's story, or the parable of the fisherman that began the chapter, what came up for you? What are *your* priorities?

Your vision for your life is a complex system, so there's no single right way to capture it. The simple systems in this chapter are a tangible framework that you can use to articulate what matters most to you. A clear snapshot of your strategic values will become the filter you use to decide which eureka moments are worth pursuing, a picture of your vision will be the lighthouse to draw you forward, and an aligned business model will keep you from being pulled off track by the demands of a system that doesn't fit what you want.

STEP ONE: ARTICULATE YOUR STRATEGIC VALUES

Every decision you make goes through a filter of your values and priorities. Hundreds of times a day, from the moment you decide whether to hit the snooze button to the moment you stand up from the couch to go to bed, your mind is picking a course of action based on the type of person you believe yourself to be, what matters most to you, and what deserves your attention. It's a mostly subconscious system that determines the course of your life. Like every system, if you're happy with the outcomes of your life, then your framework is working for you. But if you find yourself paralyzed, off track, or missing out on what matters most, this simple system can help you clarify what your priorities are and what you want them to be.

Living in a complex system like an entrepreneurial business can feel destabilizing. We don't have external frameworks to mark out where we are going and why. Natural guardrails don't exist to keep us from losing sight of why we started this journey in the first place. We have the privilege—but also the responsibility—to set up these systems for ourselves. Articulating our strategic values is a powerful first step to make that happen.

> *"Dedicate yourself to a core set of values. Without them, you will never be able to find personal fulfillment, and you will never be able to lead effectively."*
>
> —KENNETH CHENAULT

We're going to start with the big picture and then drill in from there. As a first step, highlight the twenty values that mean the most to you from this list:

- Achievement
- Adventure
- Authenticity
- Authority
- Autonomy
- Balance
- Beauty
- Boldness
- Challenge
- Citizenship
- Collaboration
- Comfort
- Community
- Compassion
- Competency
- Confidence
- Contribution
- Courage
- Creativity
- Curiosity

- Determination
- Diversity
- Fairness
- Faith
- Fame
- Family
- Freedom
- Friendships
- Fun
- Generosity
- Grace
- Growth
- Happiness
- Honesty
- Humor
- Independence
- Influence
- Inner Harmony
- Integrity
- Justice
- Kindness
- Knowledge
- Leadership
- Learning
- Love
- Loyalty
- Meaningful Work
- Openness
- Optimism
- Patience
- Peace
- Pleasure
- Poise
- Popularity
- Recognition
- Religion
- Reputation
- Respect
- Responsibility
- Security
- Self-Respect
- Service
- Spirituality
- Stability
- Success
- Status
- Trustworthiness
- Unity
- Wealth
- Wisdom[78] [79]

78 Connie Stemmle, "Personal Core Values List: 100 Examples of Values to Live By," *Develop Good Habits* (blog), *Oldtown Publishing*, accessed February 18, 2021.

79 James Clear, "Core Values List," JamesClear.com, accessed February 18, 2021.

Now that you have a big list of values in front of you, cut it down to the ten that matter the most.

From that ten, pick your five core values. Write them down:

____

____

____

____

____

If you hate having to pick only five values, you're not alone. You probably want everything on that list to be a part of your life. By prioritizing a core group of foundational values, you're picking the priorities that will prevail if two good things are in conflict. For example, comfort is great, but do you want to choose courage over comfort when you can't have both? There's nothing wrong with financial security, but in a battle between financial gain and honesty, which one will win?

My core values are:

- Courage
- Love
- Faith
- Meaningful Work
- Family

I want people to mention these five qualities about me at my funeral. I want them to be the heart of my legacy.

Having a list of core values like this is helpful, but it's not tangible. If I put this list on my website, it wouldn't be compelling for visitors exploring what A Squared is about. Big-picture values are abstract, and no one is going to be drawn or repelled by them. It would also be hard for me to make specific business decisions or train my team in line with these things. For this exercise to be helpful, we need to drill down further.

For a strategic value to be a helpful filter for your decisions as you navigate the systems in your life, it needs to have two qualities:

1. It needs to be connected to your identity and what you believe about the world and your work
   a. It needs to be so specific and tangible that it resonates with some people and repels others

STRATEGIC VALUES AND YOUR IDENTITY

A great strategic value starts with the word "we." It defines your company's culture and way of being in the world. Even if you don't have a team, the "we" includes your clients, your audience, and everyone who is drawn to your brand. What do you and your people stand for? What do your customers most need from you?

One of Seth Godin's most powerful principles is encapsulated in the phrase "people like us do things like this."[80] He argues

80 Seth Godin, "People like Us (Do Things like This)," *altMBA*, special edition, 2017.

our entire lives are mediated by this phrase—we decide and purchase and act based on the type of person we think we are. Even the brand of water bottle we buy is a vote for our chosen identity. Godin taps into that same element of human nature that James Clear did when he encouraged us to cultivate new habits by seeing our actions as individual votes for the type of person we want to be.[81]

Because the human connection with this "people like us do things like this" identity is so strong, Godin argues, "culture eats strategy for lunch."[82] Your strategic values have a direct impact on your culture. If your culture has clear, intentional foundations like "people like us rebel against corporate norms," or "people like us prioritize having fun with our clients," it can show up tangibly in your behavior, in your incentives, and what you choose to celebrate.

> *"For most of us, from the first day we are able to remember until the last day we breathe, our actions are primarily driven by one question, 'Do people like me do things like this?' People like me don't cheat on their taxes. People like me own a car, we don't take the bus. People like me have a full-time job. People like me want to see the new James Bond movie."*[83]
>
> —SETH GODIN

Start building your list by answering a few of these questions:

81 James Clear, "How to Create Atomic Habits with James Clear," December 26, 2019, episode 295, in *Online Marketing Made Easy,* produced by Amy Porterfield, podcast, MP3 audio.

82 Seth Godin, "People like Us (Do Things like This)."

83 Ibid.

- What are the characteristics of the "people like us" in your life?
- What parts of your work are most meaningful to you and your customers?
- What are people coming to you for that they can't get somewhere else?
- What are you doing that no one else seems to be doing?
- What makes you a dream come true for some people but a terrible fit for others?
- What do you believe about your industry or the best way for people to tackle the problem you solve for them?

We...____

We...____

We...____

We...____

We...____

Here are some samples to help you start thinking about this:

- We celebrate the small wins in our clients' lives
- We make every step of the process as simple as possible for our customers
- We laugh a lot on client calls
- We pay our mechanics a salary rather than a commission
- We close at 4:00 p.m. so we can spend time with our families and hobbies
- We prioritize beauty and luxury
- We believe that without strong systems, freedom as an entrepreneur is impossible

As you begin to think about what matters to you about your work, you'll start naturally thinking about things you *don't* do. You'll find things you don't like about your industry, things that get you fired up, and hills you'd be willing to die on.

Kevin Rogers, founder and CEO of a community called Copy Chief for freelance copywriters, calls this step "the Rebel Yell."[84] If you're passionate about your work or your industry, you likely have things you're fed up about. Maybe you started your business to fix something you think is broken, or get angry when people make certain assumptions about your industry, or die a little inside when someone shares about how they've been burned in the past by a competitor. Identifying and articulating those things can then become a battle cry for your business. As Rogers describes it, "What makes you and your solution stand out from the crowd is telling the reason WHY you created the solution. You do that by simply describing the frustration that drove you to find a better way."[85]

As you think about the things that fire you up, add those ideas into your list by asking:

- What are the things that light you up or get you fired up?
- Where do you want to plant your flag?

84 Kevin Rogers, "The Amazing Two-Sentence Answer to 'What Do You Do?'," *Copy Chief* (blog), accessed February 18, 2021.

85 Ibid.

- What have you experienced from the corporate world, your competitors, or companies you've worked with that you swear you will never do?
- Where are your customers being poorly served in your industry?

We...____________________________________
We...____________________________________
We...____________________________________
We...____________________________________
We...____________________________________

Here are some samples:

- We never use industry jargon because it makes our clients feel stupid
- We oppose hustle culture
- We don't make our clients wait more than twenty minutes for their food
- We don't blame our customers for their struggles
- We avoid making ambitious promises in our sales process

"One man with conviction will overwhelm a hundred who have only opinions."

—WINSTON CHURCHILL

TANGIBLE VALUES

We've already talked about why broad core values are too abstract to be practically useful; the same can be true of your strategic values if you're not careful. Think about examples like this:

- We take good care of our customers
- We operate with integrity
- We work together

Generalized values are too ambiguous for you to sink your teeth into. If your priorities are too general, they won't help you make aligned decisions, differentiate your brand, or inspire your audience. To make sure your priorities are specific and tangible, ask yourself this one question: "Can my competitor do the direct opposite of this thing and still build a real business?" If the answer is no, you're probably sharing a generally understood standard instead of a strategic value. Those earlier examples don't pass this test because it's not likely you'll find a business that has "we don't take good care of our customers" as a core value.

Our earlier examples would get much better if we changed them to something like this:

- We celebrate our customers like they're celebrities
- We will not pursue clients who would be financially destabilized by the cost of our programs
- We provide daily feedback within our team

Within the same industry, one company could treat its customers like celebrities while another gives them space to browse in peace. One college may believe in short-term debt for long-term benefit while another does not. One entrepreneur may choose to work alone while another seeks to create as many good jobs as possible.

Strong strategic values will be much clearer for your customers, too. Some customers would love the idea of being treated like a celebrity, but I for one would hate it. If your ideal client can learn about you and say, “I’ve found my people,” while others leave by the nearest exit, you are on the right track.

Do you want to change any of the items you wrote down before? If so, list the more specific version here:

We...____
We...____
We...____
We...____
We...____

Just like every other system, your values will drive your decisions whether you’re aware of them or not. When you consciously choose what you want those values to be, it’s easier to align your work with what matters to you. You can use them to make consistent decisions, lead your team, and connect with your ideal customers. Your values are a complex system, so they will always be dynamic and impossible to pin down perfectly, but knowing what you want to stand for can provide a sense of permanence in your business even when many other elements change over time.

STEP TWO: IDENTIFY YOUR VISION

Once you know what your strategic values are, you can start to paint a vision for your future. Your vision is a specific picture of what you want your Eureka Result to look like, both for your work and your personal life. Through this process, you have the opportunity to step outside our traditional understanding of what a successful business is, or how a career arc should look, and build a vision that allows you to cultivate a life that is meaningful to you.

Visualization is a powerful way to give specific color and detail to the Eureka Result you hope to achieve in your business. As psychologist AJ Adams shared in *Psychology Today*, "Mental imagery impacts many cognitive processes in the brain: motor control, attention, perception, planning, and memory. So the brain is getting trained for actual performance during visualization."[86] When your goals are vague and hazy, you won't be motivated to achieve them, but when you can mentally experience them, you will be empowered by a clear finish line and able to take real action.

Even in an exercise like this, remember that entrepreneurship is a never-ending journey rather than a destination. Your vision isn't meant to become a false summit—a place you believe will signal "arrival"—but rather a lighthouse that helps you maintain a trajectory that is meaningful to you. When you turn your best ideas into reality from a place of honest expectations, you can celebrate your Eureka Result

---

86 A.J. Adams, "Seeing Is Believing: The Power of Visualization," *Psychology Today*, December 3, 2009.

without being shocked to find it brings new horizons and challenges with it. Embracing the messy middle doesn't mean stagnating where you are—it simply means cultivating contentment in the here and now while you build toward a bigger vision.

Here are two ways you can go about building your vision: designing a vision board and creating a written picture of where you want to be.

CREATING A VISION BOARD

Even if you don't style yourself a "creative," creating a vision board can be a fun and powerful way to paint a clear picture in your mind of who you want to be and how you want your life to look. Rules for your vision board don't exist—you can create something digital, or physical; artistic, or a sequence of photos; broad in scope, or focused. What matters is that it captures in specific and image-based terms the person you want to become. If you lived an entire day in perfect alignment with your vision, what would that life be like? What would *you* be like?

If you're like me and don't tend to "wing it," one way to tackle this is to write out the different roles and categories in your life and then think about an image that would represent your ideal scenario for each one. For example, my vision board has a sequence of photos on it to represent the life I want to live:

- As a coach: Monica Aldana of Cheer
- As a team leader: a team sitting on a boulder overlooking a gorgeous vista

- As a wife: a couple in a Jeep in the middle of an adventure
- As a mother: a mother holding her two children, very present and enjoying the moment with them
- As a woman: Kalinda Sharma from The Good Wife—a total confident badass
- Our home: a welcoming brick house on two acres of land, and a young girl riding a horse
- Our community: a symbol for B Certification (representing our commitment to benefiting our community through our business), and a picture of a community grocery truck supporting people experiencing food insecurity

PAINTING A PICTURE OF YOUR FUTURE, AND YOUR BUSINESS'S FUTURE

If you enjoy writing, another way to capture your vision is to paint a picture of your future using words. Your description needs to be set in the present tense, several years into the future. Capture as many details as you can, and don't hold back with an understanding of what is "realistic." Where do you live? What are you wearing? When do you wake up? Who's on your team? How do you spend your day? What do people know about you?

A solid vision like this should be about a page long, and you should be able to visualize every piece of it in your mind.

To give you a taste of what this can feel like, here's a portion of mine:

Ashlee Berghoff is a thriving and highly respected leader of a team that works with entrepreneurs to experience real freedom and mastery over their time and systems. Her team meets annually for an adventure retreat and finds deep joy and fulfillment in working with one another and their clients. Meanwhile, they have freedom and flexibility to integrate work with their home lives, families, and passions.

Ashlee is a courageous leader who empowers her team and is not afraid to tell them the truth clearly and without apology. Her team knows that she cares for them and has their back, and that she will set a high bar because she knows they can achieve it.

A Squared Online is a household name among entrepreneurs building service businesses, and what the A Squared team creates has completely changed the conversation around the power of systems. Her book—Eureka Results—has sold twenty thousand copies, and the company recently crested $1M in annual revenues with a small team. The company invests 10 percent of its profits into social impact and supports the community involvement and personal goals of its entire team.

STEP THREE: ALIGN YOUR BUSINESS MODEL

"You are not the machine; you are building the machine."

—RACHEL RODGERS[87]

Once you've reached step three, you will have done a lot of hard work. You know what you want your filter to be for your decisions today, and you've painted a picture of who you want to become. That foundational work will prepare you to evaluate your business model:

- Does it match your vision?
- Is it moving you in the right direction?
- Does it create the types of problems you want to solve?

No business model is perfect—each one has benefits and drawbacks. But if your vision is to spend most of your time at home with your family, and you're building a business based on speaking engagements, you might find yourself trapped in a business that takes you further from your vision. You want to design your offers and your day around the life you want to build.

This can be a real challenge for freelancers especially—we're often told that our only real options to grow beyond our one-to-one capacity are to build an agency or sell information products. But if your vision is complete freedom to work nine months out of a year and shut down for the summer,

87 Rachel Rodgers, "The Math of Working Hard Once," *Hello Seven* (blog), June 17, 2018.

then an agency might not work for you (at least not in the short term). If you love building deep relationships with your clients, information products won't be as fulfilling for you. The good news is that these aren't the only two options.

Breanne Dyck, cofounder of the Visionary CEO Academy, is one of the best thought leaders I've met who talks about what it looks like to align your business model and grow sustainably. Just like entrepreneurship can set us free from the "9 to 5 until you're 65" mold, Breanne breaks her clients out of a limited understanding of which business models are available to us.[88] She does it through what she calls a high-value hybrid, which allows you to break your service into its individual parts and then decide the best way to grow each one. "Even though your product looks like one thing from the outside, it's actually not one thing," Breanne wrote in a recent article. "It happens in a bunch of different steps, a bunch of stages."[89]

When you break down your service, you don't have to pick only one option to grow it. You don't have to build a whole course-driven business when you can simply use courses to deliver one piece of what you do, and you don't have to build an unwieldy agency when all you need to do is loop in additional support for a tough part of your customer process. You can retain some one-on-one elements while automating others, or even remove steps that are standard for your industry but don't provide real value. The options are limitless.

---

88 Breanne Dyck, "Use the Impact Matrix to Scale Your High-Touch Work," *Visionary CEO Academy* (blog), accessed February 19, 2021.

89 Ibid.

Imagine you're a copywriter who provides one-on-one copy services for your clients. You spend a lot of time writing sales copy for your clients and ultimately hit a ceiling where you can't possibly take on any more projects. What do you do next? Turns out, you have a myriad of options. You can:

- Hire a team of copywriters to help you deliver (traditional agency model)
- Sell a course to help business owners write their own copy (traditional information products model)
- Automate sales and onboarding so all you have to do is write
- Delegate only one portion of your work, while you retain the rest
- Create a miniature course to get business owners started on their own copy, and then work with them one on one to refine it
- Walk multiple clients through the same stages of the process together so you can focus on each element more efficiently
- Raise your prices so you only work with a few exclusive clients at a time
- Create a copy group to support business owners seeking similar copy
- And many, many more—as long as you're bringing your clients the outcome they desire, there is no limit on what you can design to get them there

What are some elements of your business that would benefit from being scaled differently than other elements?

____

____

____

____

____

PUTTING THE PIECES TOGETHER

After completing this exercise, you should have the following three core elements:

- Your strategic values
- Your vision
- An aligned business model

Find a way to display your values and vision so you can return to them often. Paste them on the wall of your office. Set them as your computer wallpaper. Review them every day. That's how you make sure you're running the right race and will be happy with your destination when you reach it. Every time you have a eureka idea—an exciting aha moment—come back to the work you've done on this core system. Don't launch yourself into a new project until you've confirmed it's taking you one step closer to your vision and values.

Once you've done that, then you can start clearing rocks and hurdles from the road in front of you. Our next core system will help you do just that.

KEY TAKEAWAYS FROM CHAPTER 11:

- Before you make your race from eureka idea to Eureka Result more efficient, you need to make sure you're running the right race in the first place.
- One of the greatest privileges of entrepreneurship is the complete freedom to design and build a life and business in line with your vision.
- You can create three puzzle pieces to keep yourself on the right road: your strategic values, your vision, and an aligned business model.

CONTINUE READING TO LEARN ABOUT HOW PLANNING AND TIME MANAGEMENT WILL CLEAR THE ROAD SO YOU CAN TURN YOUR BEST IDEAS INTO REALITY.

QUESTIONS FOR REFLECTION AND DISCUSSION:

1. Does shiny object syndrome make it difficult for you to keep focused on a single mission?
2. How well does your business model align with your strategic values?
3. Are you ever tempted to skip this foundational work so you can get started on "real work?"

CHAPTER 12

CORE SYSTEM TWO: KEEP THE ROAD CLEAR

"If I were to let my life be taken over by what is urgent, I might very well never get around to what is essential. It's so easy to spend your whole time being preoccupied with urgent matters and never starting to live, really live."

—HENRI J.M. NOUWEN

We've done a lot of work leading up to this system. We've redefined what systems are and why they matter, and we've laid the groundwork for a healthy mindset of thriving in the messy middle, setting fair expectations, and embracing experimentation. We've also set up a system to make sure we pick the right eureka ideas to act on in the first place. Once we've set out on the road toward making our best ideas happen, how do we make sure we get there? How do we channel our time toward the things that matter most?

Sometimes, this is where the hardest work happens. Even those of us who self-identify as "organized" can struggle. We all bring baggage, shame, and old habits into our day-to-day lives that we need to unwind. I'm no exception.

I've loved time management stuff since I was a kid. Organizing is fun for me—office supplies, planners, calendars, the whole nine yards. But that doesn't mean I've always been good at it.

My last corporate job was in a fast-paced consulting firm. On my first day, I sent an email to a coworker and heard back within five minutes. I emailed the next person, and the same thing happened. I knew I'd need to step up to manage this kind of team pace. My boss, meanwhile, was an absolute badass, and she took no prisoners.

Within a few months, I was completely overwhelmed. I had just started evening classes for my MBA at Georgetown, and I was receiving hundreds of emails a day at work. I was starting to drop the ball, so I decided to ask my boss for help.

At our next meeting, she asked me what I needed.

"I have over three hundred emails in my inbox that need a response," I said. "I'm completely overwhelmed."

"Wow—that sounds awful. Let's make a strategy together for giving you some breathing space," I hoped she would say.

She did not.

Instead, she said, "You shouldn't have let it get this far. It sounds like you need to become more efficient."

So that is what I did.

I created a to-do list for myself and loaded it up with everything that was on my plate. Every morning, I would open my spreadsheet and pinpoint the things that needed to happen first. The list averaged seventy-five tasks with a due date of "today," so I learned to tackle as much as I could and move the rest of the list to the next day.

I started to excel in my classes and at work. I was constantly stressed, but I was keeping up.

I got promoted at work and was proud of everything I'd accomplished, but after two and a half years, I knew it was time to move on. I began to dream of entrepreneurship. What if small business owners needed someone like me to help them make things happen?

I quit my job in 2017. I thought leaving my old environment would help me slow down, but life moved just as quickly as I started to build my business. I pinned my hope on graduation as the day the weight would lift from my shoulders, but it didn't.

As soon as I walked out of my last class, I piled my plate high with all the things I'd been saying no to while I was in school. My new husband told me he needed a break from all the activities suddenly appearing on his calendar. I tried to do everything at once in my business too, and it took me over six months to start slowing down to a more normal human pace.

Slowly but surely, I began to understand that the stress in my life was less because of external factors and more because of my own internal systems for managing my time.

"Managing" is a bit of a misnomer, though. I wasn't taking a leadership role in my own days—not really. I was being managed by a series of external inputs and impossible superhero-sized internal expectations. Even though my boss and old job were no longer part of the picture, I had created my own seventy-five-project list in my new business. As it turns out, seventy-five-project lists *never* get shorter.

So, I started changing my system one piece at a time. I set up a project management tool and started moving projects to future due dates so I would only see a small subset of the list. I began to block off time on my calendar for projects so my list of to-dos would match the amount of time I had available. I hired help and started the process of learning to lead a team. I began to set annual goals and break down my projects across time. Each shift would make things a little bit better and lift the weight off my shoulders a little more. I continued to iterate and tweak the system as the business grew and as I began to navigate entrepreneurship alongside raising our first child.

Today, I have a simple system for time leadership that has placed me squarely in the driver's seat for my business and my life. It sets up boundaries to keep me from falling back into old habits. Because of this system, I wake up every morning to a clear, human-sized list of tasks to do. I have a small number of core strategic projects I'm working on and a consistent practice of spending time daily on marketing and sales. I have only twelve hours of childcare each week, allowing me to be present for over two-thirds of my daughter's waking hours.

I feel empowered in how I channel my time, and I am able to take clear and focused action on a daily basis, but that does not mean, and will never mean, I am in complete control of my time. I've had to rerecord videos because of barking dogs. My office looks like a tornado has passed through it (because a toddler tornado has). I often have surprise projects, detours, and emergencies that can't be prevented. That's what it looks like to be a human living in an imperfect world, and that's definitely what it looks like to be a parent. I can take on a leadership role in my life, but many things are out of my control. Complex systems (like our lives and businesses) can be guided, but they cannot be fully commanded.

I also recognize the incredible privileges I've been given by having a spouse who also works and is invested at home, enough income to hire support, and a variety of other support systems surrounding me. Life circumstances can rip the reins out of our hands, and there may be seasons when we struggle to put one foot in front of the other. But even when the world turns upside down, we can leverage systems to build some stability and support into our lives.

I don't want you to read about this system and imagine a flawless, peaceful existence where I live up to every possible expectation of an American career mother. Most of my time freedom comes from consciously choosing a different set of expectations for myself based on my values and what I want my life's foundation to be. I believe staying in my pajamas all day with a sick child counts as a day well spent, no matter what the house looks like at the end of it. I say no to many good things I would like to do. I take ownership of how I spend my time, but I also know I cannot possibly plan for everything that is in store for me and my family. I can't even guarantee I will be alive by this time tomorrow.

With all that said, my time leadership system is built to help me take focused action, protect what matters to me, and experience a regular sense of progress and momentum. It is a complicated system with a few core simple elements: two storage systems, annual targets, six-week planning, and weekly rhythms. We'll take each one step by step, but before we do that, I want to take a moment to address an elephant in the room: the shame and helplessness many of us bring to the table when it comes to how we think about our time.

UNWINDING SHAME

"I pray you'll make space to see the goodness that grows apart from your endurance."

—K.J. RAMSEY

As entrepreneurs, we can easily fall victim to a dangerous narrative that plagues our cultural understanding of what it means to build a business. Louise Nicolson, author of *The Entrepreneurial Myth,* puts it this way: "Entrepreneurial work is more uncertain, more complex, more stressful, [and] more pressured than corporate work. Nevertheless…in newspaper pages, the entrepreneur fizzes with energy. He or she is bold and creative, comfortable with risk and uncertainty, and the personification of a healthy, dynamic economy."[90]

When we set impossible expectations and compare ourselves to the idealized entrepreneur of this narrative, there's no space for grace when we think about the blinking cursor we stared at for twenty minutes before writing a tough email, or the rabbit hole we went down when setting out to do some research about a new software tool, or the pile of half-finished projects on our to-do lists. The result is a deep sense of shame. Our natural response is more procrastination. As writing coach Lisa Munro put it, "Procrastination [is] shame in disguise."[91]

Have you ever said or thought any of the following?

- I'm just not organized
- I'm such a procrastinator
- I'm not productive like that other person
- I feel like I'm failing every single day
- I'm overwhelmed every time I wake up
- I wish I had spent my time differently in that season of my life

If you have, you're not alone. We all carry around baggage when it comes to how we have spent our time in the past, how

90 Louise Nicolson, "Why Is Entrepreneurship Bad for Our Mental Health?" interview by Sally Percy, *Forbes*, July 25, 2019.

91 Lisa Munro, "Procrastination: Shame in Disguise," *Lisa Munro* (blog), March 18, 2016.

we've defined our identity around time management, or how many promises to ourselves and others we may have broken. I have yet to meet a single person who has never broken a New Year's resolution or found themselves cringing at the end of an unintended Netflix marathon. That shame and embarrassment can cripple us on the journey to time freedom.

We also live in a culture that glorifies hustle—where "I'm so busy" is a badge of honor and our expectations for ourselves grow faster than our time-saving technology can fix. Phrases like "toil glamour" and "performative workaholism" have entered our vocabularies.[92] When computers were first invented, many economists anticipated that extra productivity and saved time would create enormous space for leisure. IBM economist Joseph Froomkin even said this in 1965: "Automation will eventually bring about a twenty-hour work week, perhaps within a century, thus creating a mass leisure class."[93] But the direct opposite has happened. We've taken all our saved time and filled it with enormous expectations for ourselves and each other.

Time freedom requires routines and planning systems we commit to; it's true. But we also need to look at a deeper system—our belief system of what time is *for* and how it should be used. If we build efficiencies to save time but then immediately fill that saved time with other things, we will never, ever be free. Like we've talked about with setting good expectations and embracing our limitations, we need to pay

---

92 Erin Griffith, "Why Are Young People Pretending to Love Work?" *The New York Times*, January 26, 2019.

93 Joseph Froomkin, "The Future of Digital Wellness," quoted by Mark Ostach, *Mark Ostach* (blog), accessed February 22, 2021.

close attention to our beliefs about time and the stories we tell ourselves about who we are.

If you feel embarrassed by how you've spent your time in the past, or you find yourself thinking you aren't the type of person who can use your time well, a few things might help:

- Recognize the expectations you've placed on yourself are probably impossibly high. Human-sizing your expectations for yourself will give you the chance to win.
- Remember the amazing productivity you think others have is likely a mirage. We're all on this journey together.
- Pause and pay attention when your brain is attacking you with accusations, and remind yourself you are continually experimenting and growing.
- Remind yourself time leadership is a skill anyone can learn, and the "I'm just a disorganized creative" stereotype isn't serving you.
- Step outside your cultural conditioning for a moment to remember our "busy = good" value system is a lie.

Your time management skills (or lack thereof) have no more impact on your value as a human being than a pebble has on a mountain. Your worth is independent of what you can produce. You can set aside the old decisions you've made about whether you're "productive" or not and approach your time leadership systems as a journey and an ongoing experiment.

UNWINDING HELPLESSNESS

"Beware the barrenness of a busy life."

—SOCRATES

Have you ever said or thought any of the following?

- I want to do that, but I can't because I'm too busy
- There's nothing I can do to change this
- It's just my personality
- I'm so stressed out because my clients are doing X, or my team is doing Y, or my spouse is doing Z
- I'm so stressed out because of everything going on, but it will get better after X happens

In addition to our shame around our time and the cultural drive to never stop doing more, we can also wrestle with a sense of helplessness when it comes to our time. We can feel reactive—like we're just trying to keep up with the demands of everyone else around us.

Over the past sixty years, scientists have run a series of experiments to test a concept called "learned helplessness." They discovered animals would try to escape a stressful experience at first, but if nothing worked and they had no control over the stressor, they would stop attempting to avoid it. Even if an escape route opened up later, the animals wouldn't take it; they had internalized a sense of helplessness over their circumstances.[94]

---

94 "Learned Helplessness," *Science Direct,* accessed February 22, 2021.

Most of us have learned our own level of helplessness over our time from previous jobs, school environments, and the general culture. After years of having to simply respond to the expectations of others, our own muscles of self-management have atrophied. This is why, in many organizations, author Ron Ashkenas notes, "The standard response to any initiative is some variation of, 'we'd love to do that, but we really can't.'"[95] Entrepreneurship gives us the power to step away from our old habits, but it doesn't happen automatically.

The opposite of learned helplessness is what I like to call "time leadership." Time leadership is recognizing you have more agency in where your time goes than you think. As it turns out, no one is holding a gun to your head and forcing you to do *anything*. You don't have to answer emails every day. You don't have to bring homemade food to the potluck. You don't have to attend that charity event. You don't have to attend every Zoom call you're invited to. You don't have to say yes to every request.

If you're feeling resentful about what's on your list, you might have given up some of your power when it comes to how you spend your time. Using phrases like "I can't do that because I'm too busy," "I have to do X," and "Why can't they just leave me alone and stop asking me to do stuff?" are other potential cues. If COVID shutdowns and cancelled plans brought a sense of relief to you, then it's time to take another look at what you let land on your calendar.

---

95 Ron Ashkenas, "Learned Helplessness in Organizations," *Harvard Business Review*, June 5, 2012.

Once you step into your power when it comes to your time, you're ready to try out this system for time leadership.

STEP ONE: SET UP TWO EXTERNAL STORAGE SYSTEMS

If you attend a webinar, take furious notes, and then put everything you've learned on your to-do list, then we've just pinpointed the first thing that's holding you back: the single list. As an entrepreneur, you have ideas all the time. Things pop into your head on a regular basis that you feel like you should be doing. If all of those thoughts and ideas land on the same list (or worse, you store them in your head), a few things will happen:

- You will never get it all done
- Your list will never get shorter. As you knock out one thing, another thing will be added
- You'll be surrounded by a bevy of half-finished projects, contributing to that shame of feeling like you don't finish what you start

Sounds fun, right? There's a better way.

First, you need to recognize your brain is a terrible storage system. That's not what it's built to do. Your brain is a master of having ideas, but it's not actually meant to hold many of them. Unfinished tasks floating around in your brain use up cognitive space, making it hard to focus on what you're trying to do in the moment, and your brain doesn't differentiate well between different types of urgency or when you actually need information. That's why you can wake up at 3:00 a.m. stressed out about something you can't do until next week, or why you remember to grab chips five minutes after you leave the store. As David Allen argues in his classic book *Getting Things Done*, "A significant part of your psyche cannot help but keep track of your open loops, and not...as an intelligent, positive motivator, but as a detractor from anything else you need or want to think about, diminishing your capacity to perform."[96]

A key part of any organizational system is its ability to capture everything and hold it *outside* your brain in a way you can trust. If you don't believe the list in front of you has everything on it, you'll revert back to using your memory and always have a nagging feeling you're missing something.

A good place to start is with a full-scale brain dump. Write down absolutely *everything* in your brain that remotely resembles something you want to do. It'll be a lot of stuff.

Now, and this is key, you need to split that list in two. One will become your *ideas* list, and the other one will become your *to-do* list. Your ideas list could be a spreadsheet, or a notebook, and your to-do list can be your project management software tool or planner. The idea is for you to *know* that everything is being captured, but only *see* what is on your active list on any given day. That way, you can actually move projects forward and experience a sense of momentum.

To get the process started, list a few ideas here that you plan to remove from your active to-do list:

---

96 David Allen, *Getting Things Done: The Art of Stress-Free Productivity* (New York: Penguin Books, 2015), 18.

How do you know what deserves to remain on your to-do list? The next steps will help you make that call.

STEP TWO: IDENTIFY YOUR ANNUAL TARGETS

If you're like most entrepreneurs, you've been instructed to create specific annual goals and then break them down into quarters, and then months. And, if you're like most entrepreneurs, this isn't working for you. Why not? Are you just terrible at keeping your promises to yourself? Is there something wrong with you?

Let me say this: it's not your fault if annual goal setting combined with quarterly breakdowns isn't working for you. It's not the best fit for most entrepreneurial businesses.

If you think back to what you thought this year was going to look like when it started, and what it actually looks like today, there will probably be substantial deviations between those two pictures. The same likely holds true for your business. You've had new ideas, shifted strategies, or even pivoted your core business model. If you set annual goals and then broke them down into quarters and then months at the beginning of this year, your original plan has likely become more mismatched with reality over time. The discrepancy can make you feel behind, which compounds the problem.

What if your annual goals complemented your vision and served as a lighthouse throughout the year? Wouldn't that make things easier? That's how I approach the process as part of my system.

Each year, I set some targets for that year. They're relatively broad, like a revenue goal, major projects I'd like to tackle, or a new offer I'd like to create. Once I've done that, I write my goals where I can see them every day and review them at the end of each planning cycle.

I don't break the projects down into chunks or make monthly commitments for any of them at the beginning of the year. I allow my six-week planning cycles to dive into the specifics. All these targets do is help inform which projects I prioritize and when.

What are some things you plan to accomplish this year?

____

____

____

____

____

STEP THREE: UTILIZE SIX-WEEK PLANNING CYCLES

Six-week planning cycles are a much better and more flexible solution than trying to map out an entire year in advance. The idea was first created by Jason Fried, the CEO of Basecamp, and he has used it to build a successful company.[97] Planning in six-week cycles will do a few things for you:

- Allow you to develop the skill of effectively planning for a realistic period of time (humans are notoriously bad at knowing how much they can accomplish in a year, or even a quarter)
- Give you the space to pivot your business and pursue innovative ideas without being chained to an annual plan
- Keep shiny object syndrome at bay as you commit to a single course of action for six weeks[98]

Another perk—this is a simple system. All you have to do is sit down, pick a few things you want to do over the next six weeks, post them somewhere you can see them, and then dive in. After six weeks has gone by, you get two weeks to decompress and plan until you start the next one, leading to six cycles over the course of one year.

Here are the steps in more detail:

WRITE DOWN EVERYTHING YOU MIGHT POSSIBLY WANT TO DO OVER THE NEXT SIX WEEKS

Start by writing down the projects and tasks you'd like to accomplish over the next six weeks. You can skip any ongoing client work or recurring administrative stuff. "Check emails"

---

97 Ryan Singer, "Shape up: Stop Running in Circles and Ship Work That Matters," *Basecamp*, accessed February 22, 2021.

98 Ibid.

doesn't need to be on this list. "Clear out inbox" might be, though, if that's been bugging you for a while.

Chances are that it's going to be too long. This next step will help you cut it down.

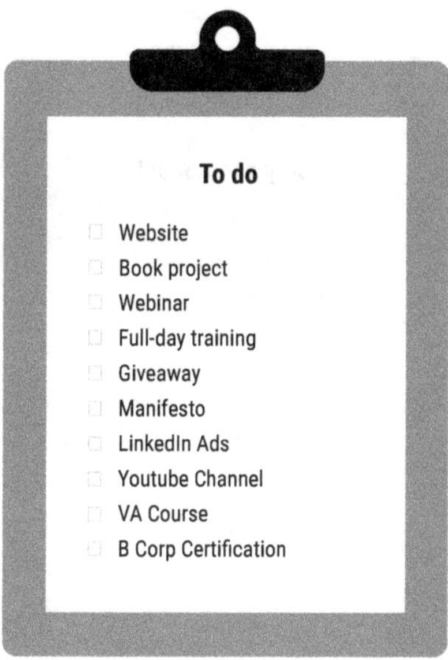

PICK ONE TO TWO LARGER PROJECTS AND FOUR TO SIX SMALLER PROJECTS TO COMPLETE

Now it's time to evaluate your list. Consider your availability, your priorities, and your targets for the year. What do you want to commit to doing over the next six weeks? Pick one or two larger projects (things that will take two or more weeks to complete) and between four and six smaller projects (tasks you can finish in several hours of focused effort).

Write down your list and put it somewhere you can see it. Anything that doesn't make the cut belongs in your "ideas" storage system so you know it's captured but it's out of your face for the next six weeks. Only a small number of projects will make the cut into your active to-do list.

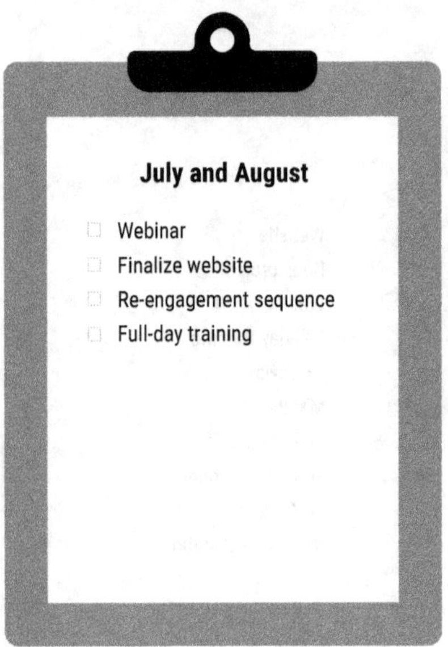

(OPTIONAL) BREAK DOWN YOUR TASKS INTO SMALLER CHUNKS BY WEEK

Some projects on your list might be well defined and granular, and you can act on them easily. Others, though, are too large and overwhelming to tackle all at once.

For example, website redesign is a massive undertaking. If you set aside an hour to work on it, you'll spend half the time trying to figure out where to start. Using some of your planning time to break up your project and decide on some initial steps will save you a lot of time and energy down the road. You could break it up like this:

Week 1: Finalize brand and initial structure; send to designer
Week 2: Home page copy
Week 3: About page copy
Week 4: Rest of site copy
Week 5: Design phase
Week 6: Begin review

This will help you see that you probably won't be 100 percent done with the website by the end of the cycle, so you can set fair expectations—but it will also help you move forward efficiently.

IF YOU HAVE A TEAM, LET THEM KNOW WHAT THE PRIORITIES ARE FOR THE NEXT SIX WEEKS AND GET THEIR HELP

Your team wants to know what they should be prioritizing in the business. Sharing your plan with them will help them all work in the same direction, and over time you can give more and more ownership to them. In my example above, two entire projects belonged to my team. I was there to support, but they were in the driver's seat. And they did an amazing job.

FOCUS FOR THE NEXT SIX WEEKS

Now it's time to execute on your plan. Your biggest enemies will be new shiny objects and ideas, but this structure gives you the tools to handle them. When you join a webinar, or see a post from an entrepreneur you admire, or have a brilliant idea at four o'clock in the morning, write down your biggest takeaways. Add those new ideas to your "ideas list." Then, get back to the projects you've already committed to. *Do not* start acting on your new ideas yet.

When it's time to plan your next six-week cycle, you can evaluate that idea objectively to see if it should make the cut. You have the flexibility to pursue it if you want, but you'll also have enough distance from the idea to know if it fits into your goals for the year.

Anything you leave to bounce around in your head will keep launching itself into your attention with a due date of "now." You'll constantly feel like there are a million things you should be doing. When that idea has a place outside your head to live instead, you can trust that it's captured and will get its moment in the sun, and you can safely forget about it until the right time.

REVIEW YOUR PREVIOUS SIX-WEEK CYCLE

Once your six weeks has run out, you have two weeks before your next cycle begins. You can use that time to pursue a fun side project, think about what you want to do for the next six weeks, and debrief the work you just completed.

To debrief your projects, ask yourself a few questions:

- For the projects I finished, what was the outcome?
- What projects used the most energy or gave me the most resistance? Why?

- For the projects I didn't finish, was it a conscious and wise choice based on changing priorities? Or did I procrastinate?
- What did I learn?

This only takes a few minutes and will help you be strategic about picking your next set of projects.

Then, rinse and repeat.

"The overachiever in us has lots of big, lofty ideas and goals. But if you want to accomplish more, you actually need to set fewer goals that you actually hit."

—SELENA SOO

Looking at the next six weeks, what are some projects you definitely want to accomplish?

____

____

____

____

____

STEP FOUR: MAINTAIN WEEKLY RHYTHMS

Once you have a six-week plan in place, you'll still need a system to figure out what's going to happen on a day-to-day basis. Calls, ongoing routines, client work, events, and vacations will often take up a good percentage of your work time. You also won't be able to work on all of your projects on any given week—your bigger projects will probably show up on most weeks in your cycle, but you'll realistically tackle only one or two of your smaller projects each week. A weekly planning rhythm will help you move those projects forward while also paying attention to all the daily work of running your business.

The goal of your weekly plan is to enable you to sit down every day to a well-defined and realistic list of projects. When you do, you'll find yourself ending most days with a sense of accomplishment and momentum.

Here's how I do it:

ON FRIDAY, PLAN OUT YOUR UPCOMING WEEK

I have a software tool to do this (more on software later), but you can use a simple spreadsheet or piece of paper to map out your week. The only nonnegotiable element is the ability to allocate time to specific projects and compare it against the time you have available that day. It's kind of like budgeting, but for your time instead of your money.

At the top of your spreadsheet, list out columns for the days of the week and add a number for the amount of time you have available to work that day.

Monday	Tuesday	Wednesday	Thursday	Friday
7	7	7	7	5

Next, add a row for calls and the number of hours you'll spend on scheduled calls, meetings, or events each day (add a little buffer if you're guessing more will be added).

Add a totals row so you can see how much time you have left.

	Monday	**Tuesday**	**Wednesday**	**Thursday**	**Friday**
	7	7	7	7	5
Calls	1.5	3	0	3	2
Total	**5.5**	**4**	**7**	**4**	**3**

Now, look at your to-do list and start allocating time for your projects on various days. Start with your daily routines and commitments to your customers, then move on to your six-week projects. You won't be able to work on all of your projects every week, but ideally, you'll work on your big projects every week and tackle one or two of the smaller ones at a time.

You can also add smaller projects into free spaces on your schedule until you're out of time.

If you're not sure how much time to allocate to various things, I highly recommend tracking your time. Then, you can review how much time you're generally spending on different projects to make your estimates a little more accurate each week. Time tracking can help you find inefficiencies and track your profitability, too, so it's a good thing to do in general.

	Monday	Tuesday	Wednesday	Thursday	Friday
	7	7	7	7	5
Calls	1.5	3	0	3	2
Daily Marketing Routine	1	1	1	1	1
Emails	0.5	0.5	0.5	0.5	0.5
Client Delivery	2	1	2	1	1
Book Writing	1.5		2	1	
LinkedIn Profile Updates		1	1		
Misc. Admin	0.5	0.5	0.5	0.5	0.5
Total	**7**	**7**	**7**	**7**	**5**

In this example, your marketing routine, emails, and client delivery represent your weekly ongoing rhythms. Writing a book is a great example of a big project (it will cover multiple six-week cycles) and updating a LinkedIn profile is a smaller one.

If you've ever walked out of Costco staring at your receipt and trying to figure out how that sparse cart of things added up to $200, you'll recognize the feeling that is going to happen next—disappointment. This will be a *huge* bummer. You'll try to convince yourself that this can't possibly be all you can do. You'll run out of time blocks long before you've allocated time to everything you want to do next week. This is normal and a huge part of why you're doing this exercise.

You will feel disappointment one time, every Friday. But on Monday, Tuesday, Wednesday, and Thursday, you're going to feel great because you're actually going to accomplish what you've set out to accomplish. You won't be weighed down by a to-do list that even Wonder Woman or Superman would raise their eyebrows at.

If you do end up with extra time (which will happen now and again), you can always get ahead on the next day, pull something new from your list, or do something fun. Reward yourself for your productivity! You'll be amazed to see your perspective shift when you give yourself the chance to win.

EACH DAY, EXECUTE ON YOUR PLAN AND THEN WRITE OUT YOUR PLAN FOR THE NEXT DAY

I still like analog methods, so at the end of every day, I spend three minutes writing down my plan for the next day. The next morning, when I log in, there's my list ready to go, and my brain is fully primed for what's coming up.

Which elements of this system do you plan to implement in your business? How will you go about it?

____

____

____

____

____

WHAT HAPPENS WHEN SOMETHING HITS THE FAN?

We all know how this goes—life will happen. Unexpected things will land on your plate. How do you manage them?

A great way to approach this is to borrow a page from the emergency room playbook and do triage. Ask yourself a few questions:

- Is this a true emergency and my responsibility?
  - If your client failed to plan ahead and is now freaking out, it may be an emergency, but it may not be your emergency. You get to decide.
  - If your spouse just broke a limb, you know the answer to this question.
- Is this more important to my mission than what's on my to-do list for the day?
  - If your hero calls you to chat, that might trump the two hours you'd set aside to write your book.
  - If a member of your team wants help with a tech problem, maybe they can wait until your scheduled weekly call or Google it.
- Can I set a different deadline for this?
  - If your doctor is asking you to fill out paperwork today for your appointment in two weeks, you can probably tell her you'll add it to your list for next week.
  - If you realize you'd forgotten about an important deadline set for today, then you might want to move things around to honor it.

What's great about having this system is you know exactly what your options are. When something new lands on your desk, you can consciously understand that completing the new task will take away a specific amount of time from a specific task. You can shuffle things around when you need to, speed things up, or cut things short—but no matter what, you have choices and can take a leadership role in responding to new inputs.

You'll also start to notice new inputs that are throwing you off kilter, which becomes a great opportunity for setting boundaries. You can train your clients to email instead of texting you, inform your team they can't just call you when they need something, and respond to emails with a clear picture of when you will be processing their request. Most emails don't need same-day responses, so if you've already used your inbox time for the day, you can close that tab until tomorrow. Your weekly rhythm becomes the way you step into a time leadership role in your own life.

***

On the road from eureka idea to Eureka Result, the day-to-day minutiae of life can trip you up constantly and keep you from moving forward. You have the power to decide how the vast majority of your time will be spent, and it's worth the effort to keep your eye on the prize and channel your energy toward turning your best ideas into reality.

KEY TAKEAWAYS FROM CHAPTER 12:

- Anyone can learn how to step into a leadership role and channel their time toward their mission.
- Shame and learned helplessness may try to trip you up on the journey to building a time leadership system.
- Our time leadership system has several elements:
  - Two external storage systems for your ideas and projects

- Annual targets
- A six-week planning cycle
- Weekly rhythms

CONTINUE READING TO LEARN ABOUT HOW PROCESSES AND SYSTEMS IN YOUR BUSINESS CAN MINIMIZE DUPLICATE WORK AND DECISION FATIGUE.

QUESTIONS FOR REFLECTION AND DISCUSSION:

1. Have you decided, consciously or unconsciously, that you're bad at time management? How can you counteract that idea?
2. Do you feel like you're taking a leadership role in how you spend your time, or are you building resentments and frustrations because of a sense of helplessness?
3. Which element of our time leadership system will you implement first?

CHAPTER 13

CORE SYSTEM THREE: STOP DOUBLING BACK

"Unless commitment is made, there are only promises and hopes; but no plans."

—PETER F. DRUCKER

As an entrepreneur, you make dozens of decisions every day—everything from huge strategic choices to deciding what to do with every individual email in your inbox. To compound the load on your brain, most entrepreneurs make the same types of decisions over and over again. Everything from "How much should I charge?" to "How should I respond to this email?" to "What should our tagline be?"

When we think about entrepreneurship as a marathon, this doesn't make much sense. It's the equivalent of turning around, running a half mile in the opposite direction, and then covering the same ground again. Every time you change course, answer the same question again, or reinvent the wheel, you're doubling back. It's impossible to avoid this completely, and some pivots are a great idea, but we can definitely cut down on how *often* it happens.

Many of our clients have struggled with this in the early years of their businesses. They would feel uncomfortable with the pricing of their offerings but put themselves through the pain of deciding what to charge every time they wrote a proposal. They would spend thirty minutes crafting a welcome email to every new client, dedicate weeks to creating a fully custom work product for them, send that work out the door, and then start over from scratch for the next client.

While my clients were doing all of this work, their brain was wearing down. In the world of neuroscience, the term for this is "decision fatigue." Decision fatigue is why, in a study of parole boards, scientists found that petitions levied earlier in the day are far more likely to be accepted than those that come later.[99] As John Tierney wrote in *The New York Times,* "No matter how rational and high-minded you try to be, you can't make decision after decision without paying a biological price."[100] That price shows up in two ways as your brain gets tired: shortcuts and paralysis. After a long day of decision-making, you're far more likely to either make a bad decision or kick the can down the road for your future self to deal with.

This is exhausting. It also turns out to be unnecessary.

---

99 John Tierney, "Do You Suffer from Decision Fatigue?" *The New York Times Magazine*, August 17, 2011.

100 Ibid.

In this chapter, we'll go over a few tools you can use to cut down on your decision fatigue. For everything you do and every decision you make, ask yourself: "Is there a way for me to make this decision only one time?"

Any time you find yourself changing a decision you've made before, pause and check back in with your mission. Does making this change get you closer to your mission? If not, save your decision-making power for something that will. Changing your logo for the tenth time probably won't do you much good, but doing the work to make your business model scalable just might.

Five tools you can leverage to keep you moving forward are embracing commitment, moving your service from custom to customizable, locking in a world-class customer experience, automation, and batching.

EMBRACE COMMITMENT

We've all seen them—the rom coms and sitcoms where someone's allergic to commitment. Sometimes, it's because they don't want to be tied down and lose their options. Sometimes, it's because commitment exposes them to potential rejection. Usually, the story ends with them realizing the person they love is worth it.

As much as we'd like to say our businesses tap into some different, more professional side of ourselves, the truth is most of us tend to be commitment-phobes in our businesses for the exact same reasons. We like having a lot of options, and we shy away from the feeling of vulnerability that comes when we plant our flag and send an idea into the world for real.

"Many people don't focus enough on execution. If you make a commitment to get something done, you need to follow through on that commitment."

—KENNETH CHENAULT

But we need to make that commitment, at least for a period of time. Six-week planning (from our previous chapter) can help you stay on a single course for six weeks at a time, and that might be enough to curtail your habit of rethinking every decision you make. Other helpful resources could be accountability (telling someone else what you're committing to) and deadlines (forcing yourself to keep moving forward because you don't have time to double back). It doesn't mean you can never change your mind, but you block yourself from changing your mind so often you end up standing still.

In her article about shiny object syndrome, marketing coach Alease Michelle notes distractions are especially tempting for entrepreneurs building online businesses because "we're constantly seeing things popping up."[101] When the entire Internet is at your fingertips all day and you don't have a boss telling you what to work on, you have to put on blinders and cut out distracting inputs. Alease personally chose to listen to only one marketing expert's content for nearly a year before

101 Alease Michelle, "How to Overcome the Shiny Object Syndrome," *Alease Michelle* (blog), accessed February 22, 2021.

letting in any other ideas. "Focus on what you know works," she suggests.[102]

What are three things you can commit to in your business that you know you're changing too often?

____

____

____

____

____

MAKE YOUR WORK CUSTOMIZABLE INSTEAD OF CUSTOM

Have you ever bought a custom-made box of cereal? One where you talked through your ideal level of crunchiness with the chef and participated in the design of the box?

Probably not—and why would you? Sure, it'd be cool to have a box with your name printed on it, made just for you. But would it taste any better? Would it be worth the time you'd have to wait to get it, or the extra money you'd have to spend? I'm willing to bet even celebrities are eating Cheerios with the rest of us.

On the flip side, have you ever had something monogrammed for a friend's wedding? Or picked out the ingredients for a Subway sandwich? Or designed a Christmas card?

---

102 Ibid.

This is the difference between customizable and custom—between adding your own unique spin on something and having it built from scratch. Between asking for no tomato on your burger at a restaurant and consulting with a private chef.

Too many freelancers and agency owners act like private chefs for their clients without charging private chef prices. They're sending detailed proposals with a timeframe, scope, and price they've agonized over for one particular person. They're providing a wide range of services across their clients, too, even though they might only enjoy one or two of them. It's keeping them stuck for years.

There's nothing wrong with customizable work—with having areas of your offer that add a lot of value by being adjustable. But if the work you do is custom made from beginning to end, I can guarantee some elements are adding extra work for you without increasing the value to the customer in any meaningful way.

Instead, you can think of your own work in the way restaurants do. Set up a menu, with clear pricing, a small number of options, and a few meaningful areas where your customers can tailor the offering to their own needs. You don't necessarily need to share this menu with your clients, but it will help you escape the trap of too much custom work. Side benefits include easier sales calls, greater confidence in telling your clients exactly how you can help them and what that process will look like, and an easy map to fall back on when you're tempted to take on a project that doesn't match where you want to go.

What areas of your business need to be customizable?

____

____

____

____

____

What areas of your business can you standardize? Think of this as The [Your Company] Way—your scope, pricing, and timeframes are all great candidates for this:

____

____

____

____

____

Here are some tangible examples from my own business:

- Our program structure and price are the same for most new clients.
- We have a list of reusable tools in our toolbelt that we can use to help our clients do three things: take clear and focused action, leverage time-saving systems, and delegate effectively.
- We work with our clients in a group setting most of the time but retain one-on-one support for regular planning sessions that allow us to go deeper with each person.

Once you have left behind the idea of custom work, you'll be ready to define a clear customer journey.

LOCK IN YOUR CUSTOMER EXPERIENCE

As we talked about in the last chapter, there are many ways you can define your customer journey. You have many options for what you customize, and what you set up as your core framework. Pieces of your business can be delivered through a course, or through groups, or in cohorts. You can make your entire business focused on workshops, or courses, or speaking engagements.

"All of our clients feel like they're getting a tailored, personalized experience. But they don't see that behind the scenes, we have our entire process locked down. It feels custom without being custom."

—TOM RAFFA

You'll never hear me say that abandoning one-on-one client services is the only way to grow. If you, like me, enjoy working with your clients individually, you can retain that element without providing a fully custom service. Just look at doctors, lawyers, CPAs, and even tailors, the masters of custom work. I don't think we'll ever start having our annual physicals in group programs, many legal questions can't be solved by taking a course, and tailor-made clothing is treasured by many people. But when you walk through the door for an appointment with any one of those experts, the process is very consistent from person to person.

You may always provide a tailored service, but if you reinvent the wheel with every client, you are bound to hit capacity quickly. Unless you're willing to charge super-premium prices, you need a way to expand your capacity without throwing more hours at the problem. That's where locking in your customer experience comes in.

Locking in your customer experience doesn't just help you—it will actually make your customer's experience better too.

I want you to imagine you're walking into your favorite restaurant. It's the tenth time you've been there this year, and everything about it is familiar to you—the music, the smells, the ambiance, the hostess greeting you at the door. Your server is attentive without being intrusive, and your food is flawless every time. It feels effortless to you, but behind the scenes, the owner of that restaurant has carefully designed every aspect of your experience, recognizing your joy in that restaurant extends far beyond the food. More than that, she has made sure the process is so finely tuned you can have a consistent experience every single time.

> *"The only two places in our culture where they really teach process and planning in addition to the other skills you're supposed to learn is the military and the culinary, and the culinary is more evolved in many ways than the military because they do it every day."*
>
> —DAN CHARNAS

Now, imagine that every time you go there, the experience is different. Not in a good way, or even a bad way really, just in a confusing way. You never know what to expect. Do you keep going back? Probably not.

Your business is no different. You can design a world-class customer experience that keeps your favorite customers coming back for more. Here's how:

STEP ONE: WRITE DOWN EVERYTHING YOU WANT TO DO ON A CLIENT PROJECT, STEP BY STEP

If you do something different every time, write down how you *wish* it worked. Keep in mind the work you've done to define what will be customized and what will be standard to The [Your Company] Way.

Add in some things you've always meant to do (like sending a bottle of champagne to a new client or calling them after the project to get their feedback):

____

____

____

____

____

____

____

____

____

____

Here's what our onboarding process looks like (yours can be this simple):

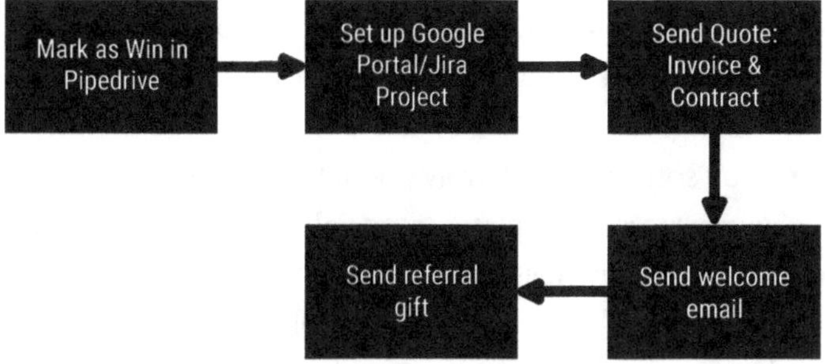

STEP TWO: COMMIT TO FOLLOWING THIS PROCESS FOR ALL FUTURE CLIENTS

Old habits die hard, and you might be tempted to start tweaking your process immediately. You don't have to be married to the same process for life, but ideally you will send at least five clients through the process before you add more steps or decide to make a step more "fancy."

STEP THREE: FOLLOW THE PROCESS A FEW TIMES BEFORE LOOKING FOR SOFTWARE TOOLS TO AUTOMATE IT

If you try to use a software tool before you've mastered your process, you run the risk of picking the wrong tool or relying on the tool to fix a problem in your process. If you've heard the term "garbage in, garbage out," you don't need me to tell you that your software tool will only be as helpful as your process. It will pour gasoline on the fire you already have going, and if your process is chaotic, unclear, or disorganized, adding a software tool will only make it more so. Also, software can be a big distraction and an even bigger pain in the butt. No tool is magical, no matter what they tell you.

Be prepared: this step will be uncomfortable. You are going to get ads telling you about tools that have revolutionized other businesses. Block it out until your process is working well.

Not using software right away doesn't mean you can't streamline your process. Templates (especially for communications, contracts, and invoices) can keep you from having to create anything more than once. These templates will also come in handy when you're ready to add software to the mix.

AUTOMATE WHAT YOU CAN

Once you're ready to pour on the gasoline, you can start looking for a software tool.

I remember when I first started my business and started to look for software tools to manage everything. The black hole I fell into was Interstellar-level scary. I found an article called "42 Top Project Management Tools to Drive Your Business" and went on a mission to discover the perfect software for me among the options in that list.[103]

I discovered a few things very quickly:

1. All of these tools had secret flaws, but you could only find them after spending hours trying to set them up
2. It was hard to get a feel for how a tool actually worked without signing up first

---

103 "43 Top Project Management Tools to Drive Your Business," *Time Doctor* (blog), accessed February 22, 2021.

3. Somehow, like magic, right after I picked a tool, I would hear about another, much better tool

All of this gave me a serious case of software FOMO (fear of missing out). What if I was missing out on something better? Since then, I've run into dozens of other business owners who are afflicted with the same condition. How can we escape?

Here are the three realizations that have helped me:

- Your process matters much more than your software tool—if your process is bad, your software tool won't help you much. You can buy all the nails and hammers you want, but without a blueprint, you won't end up with a very good house.
- Once you have a good process and know what you actually need, you'll likely find a lot of different tools will work just fine—they're not as different as they seem.
- No tool will have everything you want—the golden system doesn't exist.

So how do you ignore software FOMO and pick a tool that will make your life easier? Let's demonstrate the process with an example—we'll say you're looking for a tool to help you manage your sales process.

Before you Google "sales software," take a second to think about what you want to do.

- You gather potential clients from a weekly networking event—you come home with around five business cards each time

- You want to reach out to these people individually each month with an interesting article or thought they might find helpful
- If someone expresses interest, you'll have a discovery call with them and then send a proposal and follow up at least once for a decision
- For the foreseeable future, you'll be doing this yourself rather than hiring a sales team

Nothing fancy, but from this list, you might be able to pull out some basic requirements for a software tool:

- It needs to handle a volume of at least twenty new contacts per month
- It needs to have task reminders associated with each contact so you can do ongoing individual follow-ups
- Ideally, it could pull contact details straight from a business card

This tiny list will help you see that email marketing tools like Drip aren't going to do the trick because they're built for group marketing rather than individual outreach. You're going to have too many contacts for Excel to be helpful after a while. You can also steer clear of the $150/month sales tools built for teams because you don't need all of that.

You might ultimately choose a straightforward CRM tool like Pipedrive: it's built for tracking action steps for individual outreach and can help you organize a large group of contacts.

And then—and this is important—you stop looking for other tools. You commit to that tool for at least six months.

You set yourself a reminder to open the tool every week, add your new contacts, and email everyone you need to email that week.

If you don't open it every week, you don't blame the tool—you evaluate ways to hold yourself accountable to what you need to do. Or you adjust your expectations to something more doable.

FAIR EXPECTATIONS + GOOD PROCESSES + SPECIFIC REQUIREMENTS = THE RIGHT TOOL + MORE CLIENTS AND MORE TIME

What do you need your software tool to do for you, specifically?

____

____

____

____

____

BATCH SIMILAR PROJECTS TOGETHER

I used to think I was a good multitasker. As a matter of fact, I'm rubbish at it. And so are you. Just ask any teacher or partner who's asked you a question that you completely missed because you were focused on something else.

Our bodies do plenty of multitasking—breathing, keeping your heart beating, registering your mild headache, and sending signals to your fingers as you're typing—but those things get their own areas in your brain to work in.[104] In contrast, the executive function of your mind craves focus.

Switching costs are detrimental to your productivity. Every time you switch your focus from one task to another, you pay a mental tax for that switch. Your brain has to both shift your goals from one thing to the next and then turn off the "rules" for what you were doing to activate them for the new task (for example, if you are writing an email when the phone rings, your brain needs to use different skills and memories for that spoken conversation). This process escalates with the complexity of each task to such an extent that it can eat 40 percent of your productive time.[105]

Read that again: **40 percent.**

You pay for each switch you make—in time, in focus, in mental energy, and in stress.[106] Meanwhile, each tiny task we complete gives us a little hit of the reward hormone dopamine, providing us with a feeling of accomplishment when we're actually doing very little.[107]

---

104 "The Functional Areas of the Brain," The Human Origin Project, accessed February 22, 2021.

105 "Multitasking: Switching Costs," *American Psychological Association*, March 20, 2006.

106 Daniel J. Levitin, "Why the Modern World Is Bad for Your Brain," Extracted from *The Organized Mind: Thinking Straight in the Age of Information Overload*, published by Viking, accessed February 22, 2021.

107 Larry Kim, "Multitasking Is Killing Your Brain," *Medium*, January 26, 2016.

If you find yourself flitting from thing to thing, it might be time to start batching. If you think about a batch of cookies, you don't usually mix up the ingredients for each cookie individually; instead, you make an entire batch at a time. In a similar way, you can combine repeated tasks and projects so you're doing a group of similar tasks at the same time and removing the switching costs between them.

Try some of these things:

- Open your inbox two to three times a day, take some time to respond to messages, then close it for a few hours
- Set aside blocks of time for calls, and have at least one day each week when you don't do calls at all
- Write several blog posts at once
- Brainstorm social media content for a month at a time
- Allocate categories of tasks for days of the week (admin on Wednesdays, marketing on Thursdays, client work on Mondays)

Not only will you get more done and feel less stressed, but you'll find it easier at the end of the day to know what you've accomplished.

***

You are building a business, and that is hard work. Entrepreneurship is one of the most meaningful ways to pursue a vocation, but it's also among the hardest. When you learn how to commit to a path, make decisions once, and cultivate a consistent customer experience for your clients, you'll be ready to grow your business without burning out or making the road longer. You'll achieve your Eureka Results faster, and you'll be able to maximize their impact for longer. I promise—it's worth the effort.

KEY TAKEAWAYS FROM CHAPTER 13:

- Making decisions once will cut down on decision fatigue and keep you moving forward.
- If you're struggling to commit to a single path, pay attention to the areas where fear or a desire to keep all your options open is no longer serving you.
- Removing custom work from your process will make it easier for you to provide a consistent, world-class customer experience.
- Batching and automation can streamline your processes further.

CONTINUE READING TO LEARN ABOUT CREATING MILESTONES SO YOU CAN EXPERIENCE MOMENTUM AND CELEBRATION THROUGHOUT THE JOURNEY FROM EUREKA IDEA TO EUREKA RESULT.

QUESTIONS FOR REFLECTION AND DISCUSSION:

1. Where in your business might you be resistant to commitment?
2. What does a world-class customer experience look like for your clients?
3. What tasks are sprinkled throughout your week that you could batch to cut down on switching costs?

CHAPTER 14

CORE SYSTEM FOUR: SET UP MILESTONES

"I thought maybe when I hit that mystical \$20k a month I would fall to my knees and throw my hands in the air, tears streaming down, and feel amazing. But when I got there, I didn't feel that way. It was just on to the next thing."

—CHRIS ORZECHOWSKI, CEO OF ORZY MEDIA

I want you to imagine you're running a marathon. You've passed mile marker twenty-five and are feeling pretty strong. As you turn a corner, you can see the banner marking the finish line through the trees. It's five hundred yards away, then two hundred, then one hundred.

Then, another runner comes up beside you. She's glistening with sweat but still has a spring in her step. "You know, some people run fifty-mile races," she mentions casually. "That's what I'm going to do."

Suddenly, the finish line disappears. As you move out from the trees and a plain opens before you, you see a glint of the banner as a dot on the horizon. You see a sign next to you as you pass. "26 miles down - 24 to go," it reads. The sun is beating down on your head as the truth sinks in.

Do you stop running right here?

I would. I'd curse the race organizers, too, for their cruelty.

Everyone knows moving the goal post without taking time to celebrate an accomplishment is a great way to kill someone's spirit and any joy they might find in a pursuit.

So why do we do this to ourselves all the time as entrepreneurs?

***

I think we can all agree that moving the goal post isn't a good idea, and most of us don't consciously make that kind of choice. The problem, instead, is we don't take the time to put up that finish line banner in the first place. It feels like it distracts from the running. So, when we keep moving the finish line right before we reach it, we don't notice it's happening. Our heart knows, but our brain doesn't.

And because we're not doing any of this consciously, we can easily deceive ourselves into believing we'll "arrive" as soon as we reach whatever goal is in our mind at any given moment. But by the time we do reach that goal, we've already pinpointed a different place that will tell us we've made it.

We already talked in Chapter 8 about how arrival doesn't exist and why setting fair expectations is critical if we want to be resilient in our businesses. We have to give ourselves a chance to win and consistently remember entrepreneurship is a lifelong journey of experimentation and growth. And, as with everything else, the best way to do that is to leverage our systems—our business structure and daily habits—to make sure that happens. We don't just want to achieve Eureka Results—we want to celebrate them when we do.

You can start with three simple systems right away to experience moments of crossing the finish line throughout the process of running your business: metrics aligned with your vision, milestones within large projects, and celebrations.

"If you have built castles in the air, your work need not be lost; that is where they should be. Now put the foundations under them."

—HENRY DAVID THOREAU

METRICS ALIGNED WITH YOUR VISION

As humans, we are motivated by what researchers Teresa Amabile and Steven Kramer call "the progress principle."[108] They describe it this way: "Of all the things that can boost

108 Teresa M. Amabile and Steven J. Kramer, "The Power of Small Wins," *Harvard Business Review*, May 2011.

emotions, motivation, and perceptions during a workday, the single most important is making progress in meaningful work."[109] Even small wins can have a major impact on how fulfilled we feel in our work. The problem with this is we don't always see our own progress. As Jocelyn Glei noted in her response to Amabile and Kramer's work, "Most of us make advances small and large every single day, but we fail to notice them because we lack a method for acknowledging our progress. This is a huge loss."[110]

Metrics can help you see what you can't feel. They serve a few critical purposes in your business:

- Showing you the incremental changes and improvements happening in your business
- Aligning your impressions with reality and preventing you from relying on your notoriously unreliable memory to see how far you've come
- Identifying the things that matter enough to be measured
- Giving you data you can use to make smarter decisions

You get to decide which metrics to measure in your business. You can't measure everything that happens, and you shouldn't measure your metrics just because someone else does. Vanity metrics that make you feel good, but don't move you toward your vision, can be more detrimental than helpful. Whatever you choose to measure, make sure the system you create is something you can keep going long term. Ideally,

---

109 Ibid.

110 Jocelyn K. Glei, "How to Feel Progress," *Jocelyn K. Glei* (blog), accessed February 23, 2021.

it should take no more than a few minutes a day to maintain. You can follow a few steps to set up a strong system for tracking your metrics: identifying your core metrics, setting up a tracking system, and marking finish lines.

STEP ONE: PICK A SMALL NUMBER OF CORE METRICS THAT MATTER TO YOU

To figure out which metrics to pay attention to, return to your mission and vision. Under that vision, what does success look like to you? What is the best way to measure that success? You can also decide on one core priority for your business and focus your metrics on what will move you toward meeting that need.

For A Squared, I am very disciplined about tracking my time. It's an important metric to help me understand when I'm working too much and need to realign with my vision of spending substantial unplugged time with my daughter. I also pay attention to how our clients find us to understand how well our marketing is working; building up our pipeline is our one most critical priority this year, and it's a simple metric to track.

Every business owner should pay attention to a few core metrics, like your revenue and expenses. But some metrics, like website traffic, Instagram followers, or the length of your sales cycle, might not be as critical for you right now. You could track dozens of metrics that would provide you with some interesting information, but you run the risk of getting bad data (because you're not keeping up with them), falling victim to shiny object syndrome (because you try to fix everything at once), or spending too much time *tracking* and not enough time *doing.* If you can get the answer you need with one simple metric instead of several different ones, go that route.

Another thing to pay attention to is how many metrics you're tracking that are in your control. You'll want to track some outcomes (things like revenue, leads, or new clients), but most of your time should be spent focused on metrics you control (like number of outreaches to new prospects or number of events you attend).

What are the *outcomes* that matter most to you in your business? What does success look like to you?

____

____

____

____

____

What are the important actions in your control within your business?

____

____

____

____

____

What is the biggest priority in your business?

Below is a list of metrics many business owners use—circle up to ten that will give you the answers you need for the questions above (this can change down the road as your needs change—you don't have to commit to this forever):

- Revenue to date
- Forecasted revenue
- Business expenses by category
- Number of leads by month
- Number of open sales opportunities
- Length of your sales cycle (how long it takes to close a lead)
- The percentage of leads that turn into clients
- Average value of each sale
- Average lifetime value of each customer
- Net promoter score (how many of your customers are willing to refer you to others)
- Website traffic
- Website traffic source
- Backlinks
- Keyword ranking
- Website bounce rate
- Click-through rate
- Customer acquisition cost
- Email open rate
- Email list growth
- Social media followers
- Social media engagement
- Profit margin

- Cash flow
- Outstanding invoices owed to you (accounts receivable)
- Outstanding invoices you owe and any debt
- Net profit
- Employee satisfaction
- Revenue per employee
- Employee training and hiring costs
- Project profitability
- Customer retention and churn
- Number of customers
- Recurring revenue
- How you spend your time
- Hours spent on specific processes and clients
- How many times you engage with others' content
- How much of your own content you publish and where
- How many events you attend, and how many leads come from each one
- Speaking engagements or publicity opportunities
- Number of strategy or sales calls each month
- Number of new outreaches
- Number of times each month you offer your services to someone[111]

STEP TWO: SET UP A SIMPLE DASHBOARD AND RHYTHM FOR TRACKING YOUR METRICS

Once you know which metrics you need, start thinking about the most efficient way to track that information. If at all possible, don't set up a separate tracker that forces you to gather

111 Fred Wilson, "64 Important Business Metrics Your Company Must Know," *nTask* (blog), February 18, 2021.

information manually. Connect your tracking to the source of your information as much as you can.

In his book *Clockwork*, Mike Michalowicz describes it this way: "A dashboard with metrics will show you how critical aspects of your business are doing. Then, if something is out of whack, you can quickly check on the health of your business and make tweaks if necessary. When all of your dashboard metrics are indicating all is well, you can focus on the future of your business and not worry about the day-to-day operation."[112]

Here are the metrics we track at A Squared, and how:

1. **How I spend my time by category and task**—we use a tool called Jira to manage both our projects and our time tracking. This way, I don't have to enter a task or a client into more than one tool. Every time I complete a task, I enter it into my time tracking tool. I use this data for a few things:
   a. Hours worked per week. When it's over thirty, I know I need to trim things down
   b. Hours worked per client. This helps us gut check the profitability of our projects
   c. Avoiding task switching. Having to track my time helps me stay focused on one task at a time because I don't want to enter a bunch of five-minute logs
2. **Organic outreach**—this is our main marketing method, and I focus the most on these metrics because I can

112 Mike Michalowicz, *Clockwork: Design Your Business to Run Itself* (New York: Portfolio, 2018), 174.

control them. Each week, I print out a single page that allows me to log the work I'm doing each day (engagements, connection requests, conversations, calls, offers, posts, and content publications). Each week, I enter my data into a spreadsheet to make sure I'm being consistent and to measure my performance from week to week. I also use a CRM tool to track all my connections and remind me to reach out regularly to each one.

3. **Audience growth**—I only look at this once a month. I enter our email list size, number of LinkedIn connections, and followers on Facebook and Instagram into a spreadsheet at the beginning of each month to mark how quickly our audience is growing. Periodically, I also check out my profile views trend on LinkedIn to make sure we're moving in a positive direction.
4. **Clients**—I have a list of all of our clients with their start and end dates in a spreadsheet. I also list their source so I can see how many referrals I have versus clients earned through our own marketing.
5. **Profit and loss**—I spend a few minutes every week categorizing transactions, tracking our budget, and looking at the metrics that are tracked automatically for me in Wave (net profit, cash flow, outstanding invoices, and the percentage of our expenses that are devoted to different categories). I also take time once a month to review our revenue and expenses for the previous month and update our forecast for the year.
6. **Active pipeline**—I have a simple visual pipeline to show me who our leads are, how long they've been in the pipeline, and where they are in the process.
7. **Publicity**—I have a running list of external publicity (podcast interviews, guest posts, and published articles)

to help me keep track and share things with my audience. I also track outreaches and story ideas to help me effectively pitch to publications.

All of this takes me less than an hour per week on average to track effectively.

How can you track your metrics quickly and easily?

____

____

____

____

____

STEP THREE: SET UP YOUR FINISH LINES

Once you know what you want to track, you can pick a specific point that will mark a "finish line" for that area of your business. You know you will keep growing past that point, but the finish line exists to remind you to stop and celebrate what you've accomplished.

A strong finish line is specific and clearly defined so you know exactly when you've reached it. Maybe you set a goal of twenty customers, or a $30,000 net profit, or a 40 percent conversion rate for your warm leads. Each metric you identified in Step One should have a finish line attached to it.

What is your goal for each one of your metrics?

When would you like to reach those goals?

MILESTONES WITHIN LARGE PROJECTS

If you've ever run a race, you know how helpful mile markers are to help you feel like you're making progress. Your business is the same way. For all your large projects (and as an entrepreneur, you'll have a bunch of them), keep an eye out for ways you can set up those milestones along the way.

A few years ago, my husband and I joined my brother and sister-in-law for a journey through Norway. While we were there, we rented a car and started driving toward a town we wanted to visit. We entered a tunnel, and after driving for a couple of minutes, we saw a sign pointing back to the entrance to the tunnel. It said "1 km." That wasn't particularly interesting, but next to it, a sign pointed into the tunnel with the words "23.5 km" on it. It was only then we realized we had found ourselves in Lærdalstunnelen, the world's longest road tunnel.[113] We drove for nearly a half hour before we saw natural light again.

As you can imagine, finding yourself in a tunnel this long would be a little unnerving for some people. It also could be very problematic if your car broke down on this stretch of road, or dangerous if fumes built up in the heart of the tunnel. The road's engineers thought about all of that, thankfully. Huge fans dotted the ceiling to move air through the tunnel, signs appeared regularly to let you know where to find the nearest exit, and regular pull off spaces allowed for disabled cars to park safely. But the feature that fascinated us the most wasn't there for safety—it existed purely for psychological relief. Every six kilometers, the tunnel widened, and multicolored lights danced across the tunnel walls. Once we discovered these party spaces existed, we made the most of them with music and five-second dance parties every time one appeared.

Human beings need external validation that we are making progress and moving in the right direction. We need mile markers to let us know how far we've come, and we need to celebrate what we've accomplished. When we're building a business, we need to create these systems for ourselves.

One of the biggest and most challenging hills for me to climb has been building a platform for my business—cultivating my audience, fine-tuning my messaging, and developing a consistent pipeline of leads for my company. As it turns out,

113 "Lærdalstunnelen—World's Longest Road Tunnel," Visit Norway, February 23, 2021.

this takes a long time to learn, and for most of us, we have to put in months of consistent effort to build something with staying power. If I didn't let myself feel like a success during the beginning baby steps, I would have never been able to keep showing up day after day for the long haul. I would probably find myself broken down in the middle of that tunnel somewhere, looking for a way out.

What would it look like for you to mark each mile along the way? A 10 percent boost in a metric might not feel like much in the early phases, but that 10 percent will compound with the next one and the one after that until you really start to pick up speed.

What are some large projects in your business that could use a few milestones?

____

____

____

____

____

CELEBRATIONS

In 2013, I spent ten months in Manila, the Philippines as a member of the HR team for a field office with International Justice Mission—the world's largest anti-slavery organization. Besides the interns, the office staff were almost entirely Filipino, and I will forever have a deep respect for my colleagues' brilliance, resilience, and willingness to keep showing up to do some of the world's most difficult work day after day.

Our office focused on combating the commercial sexual exploitation of children, and my role was to help hire the investigators, lawyers, social workers, and office staff who would push that work forward long after I was gone. This was tough, tough work.

One of the things I will never forget—beyond the incredible dedication of my team members—is how well those people could throw a party. In my time there, we had dozens of parties, including weekly snack breaks as a team, monthly parties to celebrate the month we just completed, and parties for every person who left the office. Everyone leaving the office on vacation was expected to return with snacks for the office, and the one negative comment on my performance review at the end of my internship was I had missed a company family party. This was a close-knit community that knew the power of celebration.

When it was time for me to head back to the United States, I spent a few hours making a handmade card for my team. I thought this would be a special way for me to show them how much they meant to me. I showed up the next day only to find my team had made an entire scrapbook with handwritten notes from everyone in the office. There were roses. There was a feast. There were games. There were videos. I was utterly overwhelmed with love and hugs and support. Just writing this story is making me want to get on a plane.

You, like me, might have lost sight of the value of celebrations. Celebrations become part of the fabric of our communities. They help us love one another. And they help us mark our achievements together. They matter very, very much.

As the leader of a virtual team, it can be easy for me to forget this. So, I've turned to our systems. We try to have a celebratory call every quarter, where we eat treats together, play games, and recap what we've accomplished together before setting a vision for where we're going. This is a small thing, but it's a start.

A lot of companies fall into recognizable celebration rhythms, like annual dinners, birthday cakes, or bonuses. You can steal those ideas, of course, but you can also think outside the box. At Groupon, for instance, major work anniversaries are celebrated with a personalized bright green track jacket. Zappos allows each employee a fifty-dollar bonus allowance to gift to a coworker of their choice each month. And the Red Velvet Events team passes around a plastic troll to a nominated "employee of the week" with the expectation the employee will add a decoration to the troll before nominating the next person the following week.[114]

If you don't have a team, that doesn't mean you can't celebrate! Once you set up finish lines using your milestones and metrics, you can also identify ways to commemorate those moments. Here are some ideas you can use to kick off some brainstorming:

- Posting your win to social media so your community can support you
- Allowing yourself a purchase from a list of things you like
- A nice dinner out

114 Matt Straz, "4 Ways Innovative Companies Are Celebrating Their Employees," *Entrepreneur*, August 17, 2015.

- A massage
- A glass of wine
- Your favorite snack
- A weekend away
- A day off
- A deposit in a savings account working toward a larger purchase

What are some milestones, moments, and holidays you can begin to celebrate alone, with your family, or with your team?

____

____

____

____

____

How would you like to commemorate these things?

____

____

____

____

____

***

Taking the time to set up mile markers and finish lines throughout your journey will help you build confidence and give you the chance to win. It will also help you see how far you've come. I hope no entrepreneur will ever have to push through the journey of building a business without taking time to acknowledge their growth. What we're doing is too amazing, and matters too much, for that.

KEY TAKEAWAYS FROM CHAPTER 14:

- Metrics aligned with your vision will help you track the things that matter.
- Big projects can be broken down into milestones so you can feel a sense of achievement along the way.
- Don't forget to celebrate.

CONTINUE READING TO LEARN ABOUT SETTING UP SYSTEMS FOR YOURSELF AS A LEADER.

QUESTIONS FOR REFLECTION AND DISCUSSION:

1. How prone are you to moving the goal posts in your business before celebrating your accomplishments?
2. Do you tend to not track enough metrics, or to track too many?
3. Do you agree that celebrations are an important part of running your business?

CHAPTER 15

CORE SYSTEM FIVE: LEAD THROUGH YOUR SYSTEMS

"That's what we do as business owners—we're providers for our family, our community, our country, our collective world."

—MIKE MICHALOWICZ

Once you've taken the time to paint a clear vision for yourself, enabled clear and focused action, eliminated duplicate work, and set up milestones to call out your success, it's time to turn your attention to your role as a leader. Even if you never delegate a single task to another person, your posture as a leader is one of the most important areas for growth in your business. I will focus on team leadership systems in this chapter, but even without a team, you can be a leader for your clients and your industry.

Leadership is a complex system. As much as I wish you could, you can't boil down effective leadership into a checklist. You will have to make seemingly impossible decisions. You will fail. If you have a team, you will feel the weight of the fact that your decisions now impact someone else's livelihood, not just your own. Just as with everything else, you won't simply "arrive" as a brilliant and inspiring leader. You will continually grow and change throughout your career.

> *"As a leader, the first person I need to lead is me. The first person that I should try to change is me."*
>
> —JOHN C. MAXWELL

As with any complex system, you can leverage simple systems to help you learn leadership, even if you can't fully control the process. We'll cover three foundational systems related to training, communication, and continuous feedback, but first, we need to talk about the transition from "doer" to "leader."

BECOMING A ROOKIE LEADER

I learned early that the entire DNA of my business needed to change for me to build a team. And I had to change with it. After months of making every decision and taking every action myself, I struggled to let go. My business was so intertwined with my own mind that I struggled to share my vision with someone else. And my marketing was all about my own skills and experience rather than the outcome a team could provide. I had to get started and make mistakes to shift my business so it could grow beyond me.

In my own experience, one of the best (and worst) things about entrepreneurship is that it is changing me. The person I was when I started my business was different from the person I am today, and I know even more change is ahead of me.

If you are running a business alone but want to grow a business that is bigger than you, the way you think, the way you run your business, and the way you show up in the market all need to change. So, how do you make this happen? How do you take charge of the transformation you need to make? Here are three things you can start to change in your mind and approach to kick off the transition.

REMIND YOURSELF THAT *YOU* ARE NO LONGER THE BUSINESS

As solo operators, it's easy to be inextricably connected to your business. It's an extension of yourself; you're making every decision and taking every step on your own. It can be difficult to separate yourself from your business so there's room for others.

As you think about your favorite (or even least favorite) famous entrepreneurs, you might notice many of them have built personality-driven brands. Tony Robbins (a famous motivational speaker), Oprah Winfrey (TV personality and influencer), Frank Kern (advertising guru), and Rachel Rodgers (business coach) all have large companies tied very closely to themselves.[115] Aren't they successfully ignoring this advice?

The answer to that question is yes and no. Tony Robbins is more critical as a personality to his business, than, say, the CEO of Target is to his. CEOs and founders in many major businesses can operate almost entirely unseen, while personality-driven brands are tied closely to the founders.

But do you think Oprah is planning all the details for her events? Writing her own copy? Categorizing her transactions?

How long do you think the business can survive while Oprah is on vacation? My guess is it could keep going for months, or even years. Things may need to change, but the business could survive and even thrive without her.[116]

Or take the legendary marketing agency Ogilvy, which continues to function even though David Ogilvy, the marketing genius and personality who founded it, died in 1999.[117]

What does this mean for us? Here are some thought exercises to get you started:

---

115 "About Tony Robbins," Tony Robbins, accessed February 24, 2021; "About," Hello Seven, accessed February 24, 2021; "Oprah Winfrey's Official Biography," Oprah, May 17, 2011; "About Frank Kern: Three Reasons You Should Not Be Here," Frank Kern, accessed February 24, 2021.

116 Of course, not all personality-driven companies do keep going after their founder steps away, and the entire company can crumble if the founder is embroiled in scandal, but the main idea here is even famous personalities have created something bigger than them.

117 *Encyclopaedia Britannica Online*, s.v. "David Ogilvy," accessed February 24, 2021.

- If a marketing campaign you try out fails, where does your mind go? Are you tempted to think, "I am a failure. No one likes me"? Or do you instead say, "That experiment didn't have the expected results. How can we adjust our strategy to improve them?" Disconnecting yourself from your business will help you build something bigger than yourself while preserving your mental health.
- On sales calls, do you sell yourself, or do you sell an outcome?
- Can you take on the mantle of doing the hard things to defend your business? This includes asking for the sale, charging the right prices, firing bad clients, and letting go of team members who aren't moving your business forward. These things get easier once you recognize you are the steward of a business that isn't you. Your business has a deeper purpose.
- If your client doesn't get the outcome they wanted because of their own choices, do you blame yourself entirely for that failure? Or do you recognize their input while also seeking to improve your ability to guide someone toward what they need?

Where do you need to create some daylight between yourself and your business?

____

____

____

____

____

STOP "DELEGATING" THE THINGS THAT BELONG TO YOU

I'm sure you've heard a lot about delegation as an important path to growth. It's usually the first thing we start to think about when we run out of time, and there's a good reason for that. Building a team is a critical part of growing an entrepreneurial business, so much so that many people define entrepreneurship as setting a vision and empowering *others* to make it happen.[118]

But here's the thing: if your business is chaotic to the extent that you don't have a clear vision for where to go and how to get there, hiring others will just throw gasoline on that fire. They will bring their own issues with them and amplify the problem. As Bedros Keuilian puts it, "chaos is a byproduct of being human, and even the best people carry a certain amount of chaos with them."[119]

Meanwhile, if *you* are chaotic and struggle to manage yourself and your own time, unless you're rich enough to hire someone to babysit you all day, no one else can truly solve that problem for you either. They might be able to make things better, sure. But you'll become your business's biggest liability. You need to own what belongs to you.

This might sound harsh, but I want us to look at these things head on.

---

118 Seth Godin, "The Freelancer and the Entrepreneur," *Medium*, *The Startup*, June 5, 2016.

119 Bedros Keuilian, "How to Get Things Done Even When Your Business Is in Chaos," *Entrepreneur*, August 19, 2019.

What deserves to stay on your plate long-term? As a CEO, three things will forever be your responsibility: leadership, vision, and self-management.[120] You can get help, but the right support will strengthen your *own* skills in these areas. You can't abdicate your responsibilities when it comes to how you lead, where your business is going, and how you manage yourself. To lead a thriving business, you have to be willing to grow and change.

"That's just my personality" might be the most dangerous sentence in your arsenal.

What elements of your business do you need to build the muscle to carry responsibly?

____

____

____

____

____

DELEGATE THE THINGS YOU CAN

Once you've taken ownership over the things that deserve your best work, you can start to identify things that can now be safely shared. To start that process, remind yourself regularly that your time is *not* free. The next time you're tempted to do something yourself because it would cost money to hire someone else, remind yourself of this. Your time *feels free*,

120 Stanislav Shekshnia et al., "The Four Essential Roles of a CEO," *Insead: The Business School for the World*, March 13, 2018.

but each hour you spend trying to figure out what's wrong with your email marketing system when you could pay an expert twenty dollars to fix it in five minutes is costing you real money.

To understand how much money your own time costs, I want you to calculate your market hourly rate—how much you'd make per hour if you were to go out and get a job today. Say you could get a corporate job for $75,000 per year. That means your hourly rate is about forty-five dollars per hour if you factor in basic benefits. Have that number in the back of your mind, and over the course of the day, for each task you do, ask yourself, "Would I pay someone else forty-five dollars per hour to do this?" If the answer is no, you shouldn't be doing it. Even if you're not paying yourself forty-five dollars per hour, you are giving up forty-five dollars by doing this work instead—there is a real opportunity cost to your own time.

As you effectively off-load the simpler tasks and your business grows, you can increase that baseline number and train your team to do full-price billable work for your clients.

Utilizing delegation in the right ways will be a core part of growing your company. Slowly but surely, take the time to find and empower others to take ownership over everything in your business that should no longer be on your plate.

What is your market hourly rate?

____

What are you currently doing that you wouldn't pay someone else to do at that rate?

____

____

____

____

____

LETTING GO

Once you've navigated the "doer" to "leader" transition—you've separated yourself from your business, owned your responsibility, and effectively begun to delegate to others—you'll be able to let go and allow the business to grow beyond you.

> *"The best executive is the one who has sense enough to pick good men (and women) to do what he wants done, and self-restraint to keep from meddling while they do it."*
>
> —THEODORE ROOSEVELT

Alex Kuhn is the founder and CEO of Born to Lead and one of my most helpful mentors in learning how to let go. Not only does he lead a team himself, but he trains entrepreneurs how to lead as well. I reached out to Alex and asked him to share the insights that have led to the greatest transformations for himself and his clients. Alex shared some great ideas, like attracting leaders rather than hiring skills, and delegating outcomes rather than tasks. But what he said about letting go stuck with me the most.

"You need to lead by letting go," he told me. "Really let go of how it gets done, what the steps are, how it's looking. Embrace the fact that it's not going to be perfect; expect a lot of mistakes and expect it to be messy. Yet, share with them that you have faith they will succeed."

Alex went on to share a story of one of his first jobs in high school. He was working for one of his mentors at the time, and he was given the task of transporting a box filled with videotapes for a team of swimmers from one building to the other. During the quarter-mile drive, Alex crashed the van, destroying every tape in the process. The swimmers had paid $400 each for their tapes, so Alex's mentor had to refund each of them, costing him about $15,000.

Alex was on the verge of tears when he told his mentor what happened. He braced himself for the inevitable firing. Instead, the mentor responded with grace. "Shit happens," he said. "You do a lot of good work. It will get better tomorrow."

As entrepreneurs, letting go like this can be hard. Even though we know we make mistakes, too, it can be hard to accept them when our team makes them. Beyond that, we can become accustomed to things happening just the way we want them, which can turn into pickiness and micromanaging as our team grows. We have to be willing to be more openhanded with our businesses if we have a vision that is bigger than what we can build with our own two hands.

Building a team also brings real fears along with it, and Alex addressed those too. "A lot of leaders are just scared of what's behind that door," he told me. "They'll tell me, 'If I let go, then my product is going to get worse,' or 'If I let go, all my systems are going to break.' And I always tell them that some of those fears might come true. But you have to remember that you need the help of other people to achieve that vision you desire to build." When we're willing to walk through that door into the unknown and grow *together* with our employees, then we can experience the meaningful labor of cultivating a team.

As business owners, it's important to acknowledge that we have to keep the promises we make to our clients. Most people don't expect perfection from us, but they rightfully expect us to deliver according to our commitments. If our team makes mistakes that impact our customers, we can walk alongside our employees in the next steps of honesty, apology, and making the client whole. Because our businesses have a powerful impact on our clients and communities, growing carefully and thoughtfully so we can maintain quality is important, and part of that process is preparing for inevitable mistakes. Often, companies that acknowledge and fix their missteps have more loyal customers than ones that stay small out of a determination to never get anything wrong. Mistakes are inevitable whether you build a team or not; the key is how you respond to them as a leader.

What are some lower-risk projects you can delegate to start practicing the skill of letting go?

____

____

____

How can you prepare for mistakes in your business so you can simultaneously provide world-class value to your clients and respond well when things go wrong?

____

____

____

***

Once we're in the right mental space for learning to lead, we can design a few simple systems to set ourselves up for success: training systems, communication systems, outcome delegation, and continuous feedback.

TRAINING SYSTEMS

Talia Fox is a great example of what it looks like to train a team effectively. Talia's business—KUSI Global, Inc.—is a thriving leadership development training company serving government agencies and private businesses. When she started her business in 2000, she was a solo operator, serving each client individually as a highly skilled consultant. Now, she has a team providing her trainings, and I was very curious to understand how she managed to make that transition.

Talia talked with me about how difficult it was at first to find and train the right people. "When I was that small, I couldn't afford for someone to do a good job," she told me. "I needed an *amazing* job in a specific way, and everyone had to be attached to the bottom line." In the early stages of transitioning her clients, Talia lost a portion of her previous book of business as clients decided to move on. She had to learn how to train people to operate at an elite level.

The system Talia uses today is effective for one reason: it's incredibly granular. Talia doesn't train her team on high-level concepts or processes alone. Her system gets all the way down to the nitty gritty—to the level of language and energy. A lot of consulting is the posture and energy you bring to the table—it's an attitude of asking the right questions and providing potential solutions rather than sitting back and waiting for marching orders. Talia trains this kind of energy through role playing and helps her team members process the specific language they can use in specific situations. KUSI consultants are also crystal clear on the client's goals and the tactics they need to deploy to achieve them. Talia recognizes she's responsible for giving her team everything they need to succeed, and their system does just that.

Training a team to follow simple systems is straightforward. A step-by-step path to a single outcome can be captured with recordings and checklists. You can use the same process to capture complicated systems, especially if you break the bigger project down into smaller simple systems. Complex systems, though, aren't as easy to train. They can't be boiled down to a single right answer that applies to every situation. Instead, your team will need to inhabit the system for a while to learn how to navigate it. Shadowing, role-playing, and sample scenarios can allow people to watch you work, experiment, and learn the lingo of how you help people.

What are the most important intangible elements of the value you provide for your clients?

How can you use scenarios and role-playing to train your team to operate at a high level?

COMMUNICATION SYSTEMS

When I first started my business, I supported my clients as an Independent Business Manager (essentially a high-end virtual assistant). We worked together virtually, and many of the entrepreneurs I worked with had some scars from previous failed attempts to hire help. Because of this, I had to be on top of my game and a powerful communicator to build trust.

I set up a few simple systems to make this happen:

1. We had a weekly standing meeting to talk through our projects and how things were going in their business.
2. After every call we had together, I would send my clients a quick recap of everything we decided and what each of us had agreed to do.
3. At the end of each day, I would send each client a three-part email to explain what I had done that day, what was on my plate for the next day, and what I needed from them.

After following this system for a while, we were coming up on the end of the year. I decided to ask my clients for general feedback about our work together. I knew they were happy, but I wanted to understand what was working best and where I could improve. I thought they would talk about my attention to detail or specific projects they appreciated.

Instead, I heard the same thing over and over. "When I send something your way, or even talk about it, I just know that you've got it," they'd tell me. "I don't have to worry about you dropping the ball. And those call recaps are awesome too, by the way."

Through that process, I learned an important lesson about what it looks like to support someone well: the work itself matters, of course, but trust matters just as much. Reliability wasn't the icing on the cake—it was a major ingredient. I set up these simple systems to help build trust, thinking it would be a nice baseline for a solid relationship, but it turned out to be one of the most powerful reasons they were keeping me around. That sense of relief in their minds lightened the load just as much as the actual tasks I completed. Since then, we've trained and placed virtual assistants for many of our clients, and we set up these same systems for them.

When you're leading a team, you may need to train your people to provide this element as part of your work together. A virtual space requires more intentional communication than an in-person working relationship, but you can set up these systems very easily. When you do, you'll build trust faster and catch problems and miscommunications sooner.

What communication rhythms can you create to build a culture of trust?

____

____

____

____

____

OUTCOME DELEGATION

"The learning—the true learning—is in the doing. You must experience it for it to become ingrained in you. Our employees must experience the decision making for it to become ingrained in them."

—MIKE MICHALOWICZ, CLOCKWORK

Some of the most helpful advice I've received from seasoned leaders is to delegate *outcomes* rather than *tasks*. To understand why, we need to recognize everything we do has a few different pieces to it:

- Deciding what to do
- Designing how it's going to get done
- Doing it

As entrepreneurs, we tend to think about what we *do* as the important or time-consuming work. But often, the decisions can drain us just as much, or even more, than the execution. When you retain all the decision-making power and create the step-by-step systems for your employees to follow at all times, you'll find yourself very frustrated as they continue to come to you for that support. You'll be answering the phone on vacation, and while you'll feel needed, you'll never experience real freedom in your business. What's worse, your employees won't grow, either. A great alternative is to move away from delegating tasks to asking employees to achieve an outcome.

This advice has been so powerful for me because it's been so difficult. I'm picky about the details, and I pride myself on having everything "just so" in my business. I'm the type of person who naturally would want to reword my employees' emails or change the way they design a document. It's hard for me when a post goes up with a typo or someone takes a day longer to do something than I would. I often have to consciously check myself and get out of the way of my team as they do their amazing work.

When I hired my first team a few months before I had my first child, I'd been supporting several of my clients solo for a long time. We had a rhythm that worked for us, and I had a lot of deep knowledge about their businesses. I had a hard time imagining passing the baton to someone else, but I had no choice. Step by step, I backed up and allowed my team to start making decisions, then leading calls, then tracking everything themselves.

Then, two weeks before my due date, we lost a client. She was frustrated with how things were happening and saw no reason to continue. I was devastated. I thought for sure I could crack the code and get everything right without any hiccups or losses. That was an unrealistic expectation. We were growing and learning together as a team, and I am grateful for all the clients who stuck through the process with us. And here we are today, with clients who see me 20 percent of the time and are still delighted with the support they receive. It took a newborn in the house for me to learn how to let go.

It doesn't have to be an immediate process. You can learn to get out of the way and let your team grow in phases. You can move up different layers of outcomes in a business as you build trust with someone. Here is a sequence of outcomes you could delegate depending on what your team member is ready for:

- **Task:** load this post to Twitter at 7:00 a.m.
- **Outcome level one:** decide on the timing, hashtags, and image for this copy
- **Outcome level two:** create a post about our upcoming event
- **Outcome level three:** decide what to post this week in line with our event promotion campaign
- **Outcome level four:** build a social media campaign to achieve five hundred clicks to our event website
- **Outcome level five:** set a goal and metrics for social media to promote the event
- **Outcome level six:** decide to have a one-day event in March
- **Outcome level seven:** create a marketing strategy for the company for this quarter
- **Outcome level eight:** define the offers and messaging for the business

You don't need to start a new employee at level six unless that's their expertise and you're paying handsomely for their knowledge. With a new team member, you can start with outcome level one and then give them more authority as they learn. The goal for both of you is to move up the outcome ladder as far as you can.

Your team will make mistakes, but don't forget that you do too. While you're leading a team, you can keep in mind that you're letting small "bad" things happen for a much bigger good thing to happen—a powerful, empowered team with the skills born by practice to make smart decisions and become leaders in their own right.

If you have a team right now, how many decisions are they allowed to make? What would it look like to move them one step up the outcome ladder?

____

____

____

CONTINUOUS FEEDBACK SYSTEMS

When you were in first grade, how much would you have learned if your teacher gave you a pile of graded work only once a quarter?

If you adopt a puppy, do you give her feedback once a day on her obedience that day?

Then why is it that so many businesses provide systematic feedback to their employees only once per year?

Annual performance reviews without strong, real-time feedback aren't that helpful. But if you're anything like me, you're not exactly sure what the alternative is supposed to be as you build your own team.

Breanne Dyck, founder of the Visionary CEO Academy, is on a mission to change how feedback happens in small businesses. I've been following her for years because she has gone to war against many of the stereotypical and damaging tendencies of the online business space. Meanwhile, she helps entrepreneurs become visionaries who lead their teams well. I've learned a lot from Breanne, including a powerful framework for working with a team member after a mistake. Her methodology makes it possible to address problems as a leader without taking away your team's decision-making power every time they misstep. Here's how it works.

STEP ONE: INCLUDE SUCCESS METRICS EVERY TIME YOU DELEGATE AN OUTCOME

Breanne is a big believer in delegating outcomes from day one. If you provide space for your team to make decisions and share an outcome you'd like to achieve together, you can also include a clear set of metrics to define success. Your team members need to know when they have won. Finish lines matter just as much for them as they do for you.

To use our example above, if you ask someone to create a set of posts for next week, you could also give them a list of things that you'll be looking for:

- Images, copy, hashtags, and a clear schedule for when posts will go out over the course of the week
- Alignment with the brand voice and core messaging for the company
- A sense of excitement and clear picture of how people can do what you're inviting them to do
- Everything created and ready to post by Thursday afternoon

Your team should also be crystal clear on the business's strategic values and mission so they can build on the right foundation. If you outline the bar you want them to clear, they're much more likely to clear it.

STEP TWO: KNOW WHEN TO SHUT YOUR MOUTH

When you have clear values and have delegated a clear outcome, it will be easier to identify whether your employee has hit or missed the mark. If they've achieved the outcome you outlined, even if they did it in a different way than you would, your job is to keep your mouth shut about the things you want to change. If they weren't important enough to get on the list of success metrics you created, then avoid asking for any changes. Instead, thank them specifically for achieving the outcome you outlined and point out the things you liked the most.

When you delegate a similar project in the future, you can include the things you noticed in the last project. Over time, you're calibrating your own skill in articulating your expectations.

STEP THREE: PROVIDE FEEDBACK IN REAL TIME WITHOUT REVERTING TO MAKING DECISIONS AGAIN

If your team member fails to achieve the outcome you outlined, you'll have a great baseline for problem-solving together. It will be easy for both of you to see what the outcome was supposed to be and what happened instead. If you, like me, are tempted at this stage to fix everything yourself or tell the employee how to fix it, take a moment to pause and reset. Instead, ask your team member to share with you what they think went wrong and how they plan to address it. If their plan will successfully reset back to a successful outcome, then give them the green light and send them out to execute on it. This conversation should result in the team member making a commitment to you that they plan to fulfill.

STEP FOUR: CENTER ADDITIONAL FEEDBACK ON YOUR EMPLOYEE'S COMMITMENT

If the employee doesn't make the same mistake again, great! You'll keep cycling through steps one through three for new projects and challenges. But if your employee misses the mark again in the same way or drops the ball on their commitment to the solution they shared with you, your second conversation will shift to something more serious. Rather than asking a question about the desired outcome, now it's time to ask about their commitment to that outcome. Your employee is old enough to take responsibility for their role as a member of your team, and that load needs to stay on their shoulders. Your question might sound something like this: "When we last talked, you told me you would do X and this would address the issue of missing the desired outcome before. You haven't done it. What happened to your commitment to the promise you made to me?"

At this point, you're moving beyond the task itself or even the outcome to a deeper level of that person's integrity and reliability. Most good employees will move heaven and earth at this point to fix what has gone wrong. If they don't, your next conversation will likely be about transitioning that person out of your team.

Continuous feedback exists to help both of you. It will help you stay accountable to your role within the team without micromanaging or stepping on toes, and it will give your team members the space and tools they need to build their own muscles and take ownership over their work.

Do you tend toward micromanagement or not giving your team enough guidance? How can you adjust your delegation systems to give your team a chance to win?

____

____

____

____

____

***

Who you become as a leader is a process of growth that will last your entire career—it's a powerful and meaningful way to expand your business's impact beyond yourself. Even in this complex system where the results will be unique to you, you can leverage systems to pave the way for a strong team and a business that doesn't need your constant intervention.

KEY TAKEAWAYS FROM CHAPTER 15:

- Building a team for the first time will require you to separate yourself from the business. You can learn how to retain the tough stuff that belongs to you and delegate everything else.
- Setting a standard for communication systems in your business will help build trust and avoid emergencies, especially if you're working together virtually.
- Delegating outcomes instead of tasks will keep your team on a trajectory of growing independence and strength.
- Continuous feedback systems cultivate an open environment where your team can grow and improve.

OUR CONCLUSION IS UP NEXT—KEEP READING FOR A SUMMARY, EXTRA RESOURCES, AND YOUR NEXT STEPS.

QUESTIONS FOR REFLECTION AND DISCUSSION:

1. What fears do you bring to the table when you think about your role as a leader?
2. Do you tend to try to delegate things you shouldn't, or do you avoid delegating things you should?

3. What would change in your business if you loosened your grip and allowed others to partner with you in achieving your vision?

CONCLUSION

To wrap up the book, I'm going to take my own advice and take a moment to mark the milestones of how far we've come.

- When people tell you about how their lightbulb moments led to immediate transformation, they're skipping steps.
- Your eureka moments matter, but the energy they bring isn't enough to turn them into reality.
- Grit and determination alone won't build your empire, either. Entrepreneurs as a whole are pretty tough people, but not all of our ventures go the distance.
- The path from eureka moment to Eureka Result is a marathon, and systems become the tools you need to make it across the finish line.
- A system is how we do things. It's how we organize people, resources, and ideas *together* to make sense of things and make something happen.
- Because of this, systems are incredibly powerful, and we all use them every day. The question isn't whether you're using systems, but how well you're using them and how conscious you are that they exist.

- ❍ Simple systems (like addition or making toast) provide a clear path to a single answer.
- ❍ Complicated systems (like roads, or a course launch) bring together a variety of elements and other systems to achieve an outcome.
- ❍ Complex systems (like your business, or a marriage) don't have a single right answer, but they matter more than anything else. Your simple and complicated systems work together to help you find health in your complex systems.
- ❍ We've all been burned by bad systems, but that doesn't mean systems don't matter—it actually shows us how much power systems have in our lives.
- ❍ Unrealistic expectations can rob you of joy in your business. As you set out to build your systems, remember they will not turn you into a superhero; on the contrary, they will bring your limitations into the light. Human-sizing your expectations will prepare you to use your systems well.
- ❍ Entrepreneurship is an ongoing, and messy, journey in personal growth. As you build your business, you'll consistently face new challenges, but your systems will help you find stability in the midst of that process.
- ❍ Building a business is a lot like a series of experiments, and you'll never stop solving new problems and circling back to old ones. It's part of the process.
- ❍ The first core system of your business will articulate your priorities and vision so you can run the right race.
- ❍ Effective planning and time leadership habits will keep the road clear so you can take clear and focused action.

- Operational processes and systems will help you deliver a consistent and world-class experience to your customers without having to reinvent the wheel over and over.
- Milestones help you see the progress you can't feel.
- Leadership systems will help you release your tight grip on your business and show up in a powerful and effective way for your clients and your team.

THIS IS THE FUTURE I WANT FOR YOU:

Every morning, you wake up rested and calm. You glance at your phone—no emergencies there. After a cup of coffee and a hot breakfast, you get ready for the day and sit down at your computer. Next to your keyboard is a simple schedule of your day and a doable list of tasks you're looking forward to. You know exactly what the next step is for each one. You have easy access to all the resources you need, the people who can help you make things happen, and the metrics that tell you how things are going.

You pop open your inbox and notice an important client request, and then you notice something else—your assistant has already handled it perfectly. You chuckle when you think about how long it's been since you had to put out a fire in your business.

You feel calm, confident, sure.

The work ahead of you is meaningful and the best possible use of your time.

You are a CEO.

RESOURCES

To help you use this book as a field guide, I've created more resources for you. The book website—*www.eurekaresultsbook.com*—contains downloadable worksheets for everything in this book and a variety of other tools, including software recommendations and other helpful content I couldn't fit into this book.

Thinking about systems differently will be a powerful tool for you as a business owner, but you don't have to go through the journey of implementing these ideas on your own. Navigate to our website—*www.asquaredonline.com*—to find additional content, join our community, and work with us to get the support you need on your journey from eureka moment to Eureka Result.

Have a specific question? Email us at *hello@asquaredonline.com* and we'll support you however we can.

ACKNOWLEDGMENTS

I never expected something as seemingly lonely as writing a book to remind me of the power of relationship, but here we are. When I think of the hundreds of people who have invested in me and cheered me on, I realize how rich I am.

If you have encouraged me, told me you were proud of me, made me think, asked me how things were going, or gave me grace while I juggled writing a book with life in general... thank you.

Andy, thank you for loving me so well, for lightening the load, and for repeating questions I didn't hear because I was too focused on getting the citations right.

Averee girl, thanks for reminding me that there is a whole wide world to explore.

Thanks to the world-class team at Creator Institute and New Degree Press for helping me publish in nine months what I would have preferred to tinker with for nine years. Eric Koester and Brian Bies, you've created something special in this program and I am honored to have been a part of it. Rob Alston, Cass Lauer, and Sarah Lobrot, thanks for helping me wrestle too many words into something useful.

To those of you who read my rough draft and shared your thoughts with me, I don't know how to thank you. Andrey Ivanov, Brad Eisenberg, Joanna Platt, and John Holcroft, you invested in me and in this book, and I am deeply grateful. Grampie and Dad, it means the world to me that I made you proud.

Thank you so much to those of you who took the time to share your story with me or allowed me to share your story through my book:

- Alex Kuhn (Leadership Mentor and Founder of Born to Lead; *https://alex-kuhn.com/*)
- Amanda Keating (Founder and Psychologist at Dr. Keating and Associates; *http://www.amandakeating.com/*)
- Andie Davidson (Founder and Educator at Journey Academy; *https://journeyacademycolorado.com/*)
- Ash Ambirge (Author and Founder of the Middle Finger Project; *https://www.themiddlefingerproject.org/*)
- Breanne Dyck (Co-Founder of Visionary CEO Academy; *https://visionaryceoacademy.com/*)
- Caroline Mays (Founder and Bio Writer at Switchblade Lemonade; *https://switchbladelemonade.com/*)
- Chris Orzechowski (CEO and Creative Director at Orzy Media; *https://orzymedia.com/*)
- Christa Davis (Founder and Business Coach; *https://christadaviscoaching.com/*)

- Cindy Gasior (Founder of Transitions Home Staging; *https://transitionshomestagingtulsa.com/*)
- Dean Edelson (Direct Response Copywriter; *http://www.1bigideamarketing.com/*)
- Erna Blooms (Brand Expert, Growth Action Coach, Founder of Blooming Aces; *https://bloomingaces.com/*)
- Ivan Mladenovic (Founder and CEO of Preemo; *https://preemo.com/*)
- Jen Dalton (Founder and Brand Strategist at Brand Mirror; *http://www.brandmirror.com/*)
- Jen O'Deay (Founder and Copywriter at Feel These Words; *https://feelthesewords.com/*)
- Joanna Platt (Founder and Life Coach; *https://joanna-platt.com/*)
- Josh Massey (Co-Founder and Financial Intelligence Coach at Ortus Academy; *https://www.ortusacademy.com/*)
- Katherine Doble (President and Marketing Data Analyst at Ingage; *https://www.ingage.biz/*)
- Laura Gale (Author and Ghostwriter; *https://lauraiswriting.com/*)
- Marie Sotelo (B2B Copywriter and Legal Educator to Freelancers; *http://mariesotelo.com/*)
- Martin Cunningham (Justice Sector Reform Expert, Executive Coach and Founder of Competency Based Interviews; *https://www.linkedin.com/in/martincunningham1/*)
- Maryann Lombardi (Associate Director at the DC Office of Creative Affairs; *https://www.maryannlombardi.com/*)
- Mary Barbee (Director of Operations at Copy Chief; *https://copychief.com/*)

- Mary Grace Gardner (Founder and College Admissions and Career Coach at The Young Professionista; *https://www.theyoungprofessionista.com/*)
- Rachel Mazza (Sales Funnel Consultant and Chief Marketing Officer at Copy Chief; *https://copychief.com*)
- Shannon Larkins (Founder and Brand Strategist at Blackcoffee; *https://blackcoffeestudio.com/*)
- Shelly Davies (Rockstar Writer-Trainer and Joyful Badass; *https://www.shellydavies.com*)
- Stephanie Hayes (Founder and Business Strategist; *https://www.stephaniehayes.biz/*)
- Talia Fox (Founder and Leadership Strategist at KUSI Global, Inc.; *https://kusitraining.com/*)
- Tom Aronica (Founder and CEO of Biller Genie; *https://billergenie.com/*)
- Tom Raffa (Founder of Raffa and National Leader of the Nonprofit and Social Sector Group at Marcum; *https://www.marcumllp.com/*)
- Vicki Moore (Learning and Development Consultant and Founder at Moore Learning Solutions; *https://moorelearningsolutions.com/*)
- Vicky Quinn (Founder and Author Coach at Moxie Books; *https://moxiebooks.co.uk/*)
- Walt Gasior (Co-Owner of Transitions Home Staging; *https://transitionshomestagingtulsa.com/*)

Special thanks are due to my biggest supporters:

- Patrick Lee and Theresa Connelly, who went above and beyond to make sure this book can get into as many hands as possible. (Find them at *www.chesapeakethinktank.com.*)

- Paul and Suzee Stafford, a.k.a. Mom and Dad, for investing in my work and taking me seriously even though you had started several businesses before I was out of diapers. (Find Paul at *www.allies21.com.*)
- Gabriela Bell, founder of Organized Q, who has been a friend and inspiration throughout this process and a champion of the book. (Find her at *www.organizedq.com.*)

To the over seventy of you who chose to support the book long before you could read it, you're amazing. A huge thank you to:

- Alex Kuhn
- Alyssa Twist Light
- Amanda Clinton
- Amanda Keating
- Andy and Averee Berghoff
- Angie Colee
- Benjamin and Emily Albaugh
- Biorn Falcken
- BJ Pivonka
- Bobby Kegley
- Brad Eisenberg
- Brendan English
- Carrie Do
- Chris Orzechowski
- Christa Davis
- Christina Pinnell Rawls
- Christine Roddy
- Christy Batta
- Colin Campbell
- Daniel and Jodie Kim

- DeDee Cai
- Eric Koester
- Erika Dunham
- Esther and Noah Seto
- Evan Kirsch
- Georgia Loftis
- Guillermo Rubio
- Janette Gallardo
- Jason and Marci Campbell
- Jay Kenny
- Jeff Reid
- Jen Keene
- Jesse Scharff
- Jim and Susan Berghoff
- Joe and Kayla Berghoff
- John Holcroft
- Josh Massey
- Joshua Schwartz
- Josiah and Lindsey Swinborne
- Julie Hassett
- Kenton and Jaimie Mattoon
- Kevin Papke
- Kim Levone
- Kyle and Jamie Johnson
- Laura Richards
- Martin Cunningham
- Mary Campbell
- Mason and Emma Stafford
- Maureen Nguyen
- Meagan LaBossiere
- Megan and Andrew Rolander
- Megan and Jed Mahan

- Michael King
- Neal Salzman
- Pete and Joanie Peterson
- Phil and Blaine Stafford
- Rachel Mazza
- Rachel Pugliese
- Rosie Moore
- Selena Tramayne
- Sheila Long
- Shye Gilad
- Steve Krakower
- Tadina Ross
- Troy and Kaye Stafford
- Vicki Moore
- Vicky Quinn
- Walt and Cindy Gasior

APPENDIX

INTRODUCTION

Godlewski, Nina. "Small Business Revenue Statistics (2021): Annual Sales and Earnings." Fundera, last modified December 16, 2020. *https://www.fundera.com/resources/small-business-revenue-statistics.*

McIntyre, Georgia. "What Percentage of Small Businesses Fail? (and Other Need-to-Know Stats)." Fundera (blog), last modified November 20, 2020. *https://www.fundera.com/blog/what-percentage-of-small-businesses-fail.*

CHAPTER 1

Brooks, David. The Road to Character. New York: Random House Trade Paperbacks, 2016.

Grossman, David. "Study Shows Precisely How Nazi Infrastructure Enabled the Worst of the Holocaust." Popular Mechanics. January 2, 2019. *https://www.popularmechanics.com/military/a25725350/nazi-infrastructure-holocaust-lewi-stone/.*

The Guardian. "Signs of German Antisemitism Before Hitler." September 9, 2009. *https://www.theguardian.com/world/2009/sep/09/german-antisemitism-holocaust-second-world-war.*

History.com. "Armenian Genocide." October 31, 2019. *https://www.history.com/topics/world-war-i/armenian-genocide.*

History.com. "Eugenics." October 28, 2019. *https://www.history.com/topics/germany/eugenics.*

Hughes-Hallett, Lucy. "Fear, Shame, Guilt, Suicide: Ordinary Germans at the End of the Second World War." NewStatesman. August 21, 2019. *https://www.newstatesman.com/culture/books/2019/08/fear-shame-guilt-suicide-ordinary-germans-end-second-world-war.*

Lexico.com. s.v. "System." Oxford University Press, 2020. *https://www.lexico.com/definition/system.*

Llewellyn, Jennifer, Jim Southey, and Steve Thompson. "The Nazi Economic Recovery." Alpha History. July 16, 2020. *https://alphahistory.com/nazigermany/nazi-economic-recovery.*

National Institute for Health Care Management Foundation. "Systemic Racism & Health Care, COVID & Treatment." Accessed February 12, 2021. *https://nihcm.org/publications/systemic-racism-health-care-covid-treatment.*

Nederman, Cary. s.v. "Individualism." New Dictionary of the History of Ideas. Encyclopedia.com. Accessed February 12, 2021. *https://www.encyclopedia.com/history/dictionaries-thesauruses-pictures-and-press-releases/individualism-0*

Watts, Edward J. "The Fall of Rome and the Lessons for America." Time. December 15, 2018. *https://time.com/5478197/the-fall-of-rome-and-the-lessons-for-america/.*

Weeks, Linton. "Defeating Polio, the Disease That Paralyzed America." NPR History Dept. April 10, 2015. *https://www.npr.org/sections/npr-history-dept/2015/04/10/398515228/defeating-the-disease-that-paralyzed-america.*

CHAPTER 2

Feld, Brad. "Simple, Complicated, and Complex Systems." Feld Thoughts (blog). March 28, 2019. *https://feld.com/archives/2019/03/simple-complicated-and-complex-systems.html.*

Snowden, David J., and Mary E. Boone. "A Leader's Framework for Decision Making." Harvard Business Review. November 2007. *https://hbr.org/2007/11/a-leaders-framework-for-decision-making.*

CHAPTER 3

BrainFlow. "Inside Tim Ferriss' Morning Routine: The 5-Step Process to Win the Day." Accessed February 12, 2021. *https://brainflow.co/index.php/2018/01/04/tim-ferriss-morning-routine/.*

The Chalkboard. "The Truth about Working from Home: 7 Keys for a More Beautiful + Productive Workspace." Accessed February 12, 2021. *https://thechalkboardmag.com/rachel-rodgers-advice.*

Clockify. "Daily Routines and Habits of Highly Productive People." Accessed February 12, 2021. *https://clockify.me/daily-routines-habits-productive-people.*

Covey, Stephen R. "Big Rocks." Franklin Covey. Video, 04:01. *https://resources.franklincovey.com/the-8th-habit/big-rocks-stephen-r-covey.*

Dave, Kaivan. "Daily Morning Routine Habits of Successful CEOs." Awesome Coffee. October 7, 2020. *https://awesomecoffee.com/blogs/morning-routine/successful-ceos-routines.*

Elmansy, Rafiq. "The Six Systems Thinking Steps to Solve Complex Problems." Designorate (blog). February 9, 2016. *https://www.designorate.com/systems-thinking-steps-solve-complex-problems/.*

Feld, Brad. "Life Dinner." Feld Thoughts (blog). March 7, 2008. *https://feld.com/archives/2008/03/life-dinner.html.*

Gale, Laura. Email message. November 27, 2020.

Kruse, Kevin. "The Jack Dorsey Productivity Secret That Enables Him to Run Two Companies at Once." Forbes. October 12, 2015. *https://www.forbes.com/sites/kevinkruse/2015/10/12/jack-dorsey-productivity-secret/?sh=7cf50725136a.*

Nugent, Annabel. "Tried and Tested: 3 Daily Routines of Mega-Successful Women." XCityPlus. March 2020. *https://xcityplus.com/features/7188/daily-routines-of-3-successful-women-journalism/.*

Winfrey, Oprah. "What Oprah Knows for Sure about Finding the Fullest Expression of Yourself." O, The Oprah Magazine. February 2012. *http://www.oprah.com/health/oprah-on-stillness-and-meditation-oprah-visits-fairfield-iowa.*

Yang, Suttida. "50 Inspirational Quotes of Black Entrepreneurs & Leaders." Suttida Yang (blog). June 11, 2020. *https://suttidayang.com/50-inspirational-quotes-of-black-entrepreneurs-leaders/.*

CHAPTER 4

Levitin, Daniel J. "Why the Modern World Is Bad for Your Brain." The Guardian. January 18, 2015. *https://www.theguardian.*

com/science/2015/jan/18/modern-world-bad-for-brain-daniel-j-levitin-organized-mind-information-overload.

Michalowicz, Mike. Clockwork: Design Your Business to Run Itself. New York: Portfolio, 2018.

Sargut, Gökçe, and Rita Gunther McGrath. "Learning to Live with Complexity." Harvard Business Review. September 2011. *https://hbr.org/2011/09/learning-to-live-with-complexity.*

CHAPTER 5

The Agile Alliance. "Manifesto for Agile Software Development." 2001. *https://agilemanifesto.org/.*

García, Héctor, and Francesc Miralles. Ikigai: The Japanese Secret to a Long and Happy Life. New York: Penguin, 2016.

Haslam, Andrew. "Luther's Advice: Concentrate When You Pray." Think. September 10, 2015. *https://thinktheology.co.uk/blog/article/luthers_advice_concentrate_when_you_pray.*

Highsmith, Jim. "History: The Agile Manifesto." The Agile Alliance. 2001. *https://agilemanifesto.org/history.html.*

Mogi, Ken. "This Japanese Secret to a Longer and Happier Life Is Gaining Attention from Millions Around the World." CNBC. May 22, 2019. *https://www.cnbc.com/2019/05/22/the-japanese-secret-to-a-longer-and-happier-life-is-gaining-attention-from-millions.html.*

Tate, Garik. "Arianna Huffington Talks Meditation, the Importance of Failure, and the Underrated Power of Sleep." High Existence. Accessed March 3, 2021. *https://highexistence.com/arianna-huffington-interview/.*

CHAPTER 6

Buchanan, Laurie. "Tuesdays with Laurie." Tuesdays with Laurie (blog). Last updated November 24, 2020. *https://tuesdayswith-laurie.com/.*

Bucy, Michael, Adrian Finlayson, Greg Kelly, and Chris Moye. "The 'How' of Transformation." McKinsey and Company. May 9, 2016. *https://www.mckinsey.com/industries/retail/our-insights/the-how-of-transformation.*

Harris, Tristan. The Social Dilemma. Film. Directed by Jeff Orlowski. Atlanta: Exposure Labs, 2020. Streaming.

Ollhoff, Jim, and Michael Walcheski. "Making the Jump to Systems Thinking." The Systems Thinker. Accessed February 13, 2021. *https://thesystemsthinker.com/making-the-jump-to-systems-thinking/.*

Spiek, Chris. "Unpacking the Progress Making Forces Diagram." JTBD Radio (blog). February 23, 2012. *http://jobstobedone.org/radio/unpacking-the-progress-making-forces-diagram/.*

Yeung, Jessie, and Luke McGee. "What We Know about the Beirut Blast." CNN. August 6, 2020. *https://www.cnn.com/2020/08/05/middleeast/beirut-blast-explainer-intl-hnk/index.html.*

CHAPTER 7

Godin, Seth. The Dip. New York: Portfolio, 2007.

CHAPTER 8

Collins, Jim. "The Stockdale Paradox." JimCollins.com. Accessed February 15, 2021. *https://www.jimcollins.com/media_topics/TheStockdaleParadox.html.*

Merton, Thomas. No Man Is an Island. New York: Houghton Mifflin Harcourt Publishing Company, 1983.

Visit Colorado Springs. "Manitou Incline: Tourist Cable Car Track Turned Heart-Pounding Workout!" Accessed February 15, 2021. *https://www.visitcos.com/things-to-do/outdoors/manitou-incline-near-colorado-springs-colorado/.*

Von Bergen, C. W., and Martin S. Bressler. "How Managers Use the Stockdale Paradox to Balance 'the Now and the Next'." Administrative Issues Journal: Connecting Education, Practice, and Research 7, no. 2 (winter 2017): 70–80. *https://doi.org/10.5929/2017.7.2.1.*

CHAPTER 9

Ambirge, Ash. "The 67 Emotions of Unconventional Success: My Story." The Middle Finger Project (blog). December 3, 2010.

Ambirge, Ash. The Middle Finger Project: Trash Your Imposter Syndrome and Live the Unf*ckwithable Life You Deserve. New York: Portfolio, 2020.

Clear, James. "3-2-1: On Systems vs. Goals, Identity-Based Habits, and the Lessons of Life." JamesClear.com. January 2, 2020. *https://jamesclear.com/3-2-1/january-2-2020.*

Clear, James. "How to Create Atomic Habits with James Clear." December 26, 2019. Episode 295. In Online Marketing Made Easy. Produced by Amy Porterfield. Podcast. MP3 audio. *http://*

amyporterfield.omme.libsynpro.com/295-how-to-create-atomic-habits-with-james-clear.

Wicks, Robert. "Outflank Your Own Resistances to Change," Psychology Today, September 14, 2009. *https://www.psychologytoday.com/us/blog/the-resilient-life/200909/outflank-your-own-resistances-change.*

CHAPTER 10

Brown, Brené. Call to Courage. Directed by Sandra Restrepo. (Los Gatos, Netflix, 2019). Streaming.

Kasabian, Paul. "Michael Jordan's Worst Career Game Stats, Shooting Performances and Misses." Bleacher Report. May 10, 2020. *https://bleacherreport.com/articles/2890494-michael-jordans-worst-career-game-stats-shooting-performances-and-misses.*

Kumar, Ram. "The Greatest Inventor 'Thomas Alva Edison's' Vision on Failures." Medium. December 29, 2019. *https://medium.com/@ramkumarhq/the-greatest-inventor-thomas-alva-edisons-vision-on-failures-b6df41b5d715.*

Pilon, Annie. "21 Entrepreneurs Who Failed Big Before Becoming a Success." Small Business Trends. Last updated November 2, 2017. *https://smallbiztrends.com/2016/01/entrepreneurs-who-failed.html.*

CHAPTER 11

Adams, A.J. "Seeing Is Believing: The Power of Visualization." Psychology Today. December 3, 2009. *https://www.psychologytoday.com/us/blog/flourish/200912/seeing-is-believing-the-power-visualization.*

Carver, Courtney. "The Story of the Mexican Fisherman." The Simplicity Space (blog). Accessed February 18, 2021. *https://bemorewithless.com/the-story-of-the-mexican-fisherman/.*

Clear, James. "Core Values List." JamesClear.com. Accessed February 18, 2021. *https://jamesclear.com/core-values.*

Clear, James. "How to Create Atomic Habits with James Clear." December 26, 2019. Episode 295. In Online Marketing Made Easy. Produced by Amy Porterfield. Podcast. MP3 audio. *http://amyporterfield.omme.libsynpro.com/295-how-to-create-atomic-habits-with-james-clear.*

Dyck, Breanne. "Use the Impact Matrix to Scale Your High-Touch Work." Visionary CEO Academy (blog). Accessed February 19, 2021. *https://visionaryceoacademy.com/high-touch/.*

Ferriss, Tim. The Four-Hour Work Week. New York: Harmony Books, 2009.

Godin, Seth. "People like Us (Do Things like This)." altMBA. Special edition. 2017. *https://seths.blog/wp-content/uploads/2013/07/2017-people-like-us.pdf.*

Jackson, Dean. "Life Behind the Scenes with Dean Jackson and James Schramko—Part 6 of 25—Time Secrets." December 5, 2019. In SuperFast Business. Produced by James Schramko. Podcast. MP3 audio. *https://www.superfastbusiness.com/business/701-life-behind-the-scenes-with-dean-jackson-and-james-schramko-part-6-of-25-time-secrets/.*

Rodgers, Rachel. "The Math of Working Hard Once." Hello Seven. June 17, 2018. *https://helloseven.co/the-math-of-working-hard-once/.*

Rogers, Kevin. "The Amazing Two-Sentence Answer to 'What Do You Do?'." Copy Chief (blog). Accessed February 18, 2021. *https://copychief.com/rebel-yell/.*

Stemmle, Connie. "Personal Core Values List: 100 Examples of Values to Live By." Develop Good Habits (blog). Oldtown Publishing. Accessed February 18, 2021. *https://www.developgoodhabits.com/core-values/.*

CHAPTER 12

Allen, David. Getting Things Done: The Art of Stress-Free Productivity. New York: Penguin Books, 2015.

Ashkenas, Ron. "Learned Helplessness in Organizations." Harvard Business Review. June 5, 2012. *https://hbr.org/2012/06/learned-helplessness-in-organi.*

Froomkin, Joseph. "The Future of Digital Wellness." Quoted by March Ostach. Mark Ostach (blog). Accessed February 22, 2021. *https://markostach.com/the-future-of-digital-wellness/.*

Griffith, Erin. "Why Are Young People Pretending to Love Work?" The New York Times. January 26, 2019. *https://www.nytimes.com/2019/01/26/business/against-hustle-culture-rise-and-grind-tgim.html.*

Munro, Lisa. "Procrastination: Shame in Disguise." Lisa Munro (blog). March 18, 2016. *http://www.lisamunro.net/blog-1/2016/3/18/ri69q01g03q6zig4ug6jfsst1iy41q.*

Nicolson, Louise. "Why Is Entrepreneurship Bad for Our Mental Health?" Interview by Sally Percy. Forbes. July 25, 2019. *https://www.forbes.com/sites/sallypercy/2019/07/25/why-is-entrepreneurship-bad-for-our-mental-health.*

Science Direct. "Learned Helplessness." Accessed February 22, 2021. *https://www.sciencedirect.com/topics/neuroscience/learned-helplessness.*

Singer, Ryan. "Shape up: Stop Running in Circles and Ship Work That Matters." Basecamp. Accessed February 22, 2021. *https://basecamp.com/shapeup/webbook.*

CHAPTER 13

American Psychological Association. "Multitasking: Switching Costs." March 20, 2006. *https://www.apa.org/research/action/multitask.*

The Human Origin Project. "The Functional Areas of the Brain." Accessed February 22, 2021. *https://humanoriginproject.com/functional-areas-of-brain/.*

Kim, Larry. "Multitasking Is Killing Your Brain." Medium. January 26, 2016. *https://medium.com/the-mission/multitasking-is-killing-your-brain-79104e62e930.*

Levitin, Daniel J. "Why the Modern World Is Bad for Your Brain." Extracted from The Organized Mind: Thinking Straight in the Age of Information Overload. Published by Viking. Accessed February 22, 2021. *https://www.theguardian.com/science/2015/jan/18/modern-world-bad-for-brain-daniel-j-levitin-organized-mind-information-overload.*

Michelle, Alease. "How to Overcome the Shiny Object Syndrome." Alease Michelle (blog). Accessed February 22, 2021. *http://aleasemichelle.com/how-to-overcome-the-shiny-object-syndrome/.*

Tierney, John. "Do You Suffer from Decision Fatigue?" The New York Times Magazine. August 17, 2011. *https://www.nytimes.*

com/2011/08/21/magazine/do-you-suffer-from-decision-fatigue.html.

Time Doctor (blog). "43 Top Project Management Tools to Drive Your Business." Accessed February 22, 2021. *https://biz30.timedoctor.com/guide/project-management-tools/.*

CHAPTER 14

Amabile, Teresa M., and Steven J. Kramer. "The Power of Small Wins." Harvard Business Review. May 2011. *https://hbr.org/2011/05/the-power-of-small-wins.*

Glei, Jocelyn K. "How to Feel Progress." Jocelyn K. Glei (blog). Accessed February 23, 2021. *https://jkglei.com/progress/.*

Michalowicz, Mike. Clockwork: Design Your Business to Run Itself. New York: Portfolio, 2018.

Straz, Matt. "4 Ways Innovative Companies Are Celebrating Their Employees." Entrepreneur. August 17, 2015. *https://www.entrepreneur.com/article/249460.*

Visit Norway. "Lærdalstunnelen—World's Longest Road Tunnel." February 23, 2021. *https://www.visitnorway.com/listings/l%C3%A6rdalstunnelen-worlds-longest-road-tunnel/12205/#:~:text=At%2024.5%20kilometres%2C%20the%20L%C3%A6rdal,connection%20between%20Oslo%20and%20Bergen.*

Wilson, Fred. "64 Important Business Metrics Your Company Must Know." nTask (blog). February 18, 2021. *https://www.ntaskmanager.com/blog/business-metrics/.*

CHAPTER 15

Encyclopaedia Britannica Online. s.v. "David Ogilvy." Accessed February 24, 2021. *https://www.britannica.com/biography/David-Ogilvy.*

Godin, Seth. "The Freelancer and the Entrepreneur." Medium. The Startup. June 5, 2016. *https://medium.com/swlh/the-freelancer-and-the-entrepreneur-c79d2bbb52b2.*

Hello Seven. "About." Accessed February 24, 2021. *https://helloseven.co/about/.*

Kern, Frank. "About Frank Kern: Three Reasons You Should Not Be Here." Accessed February 24, 2021. *https://frankkern.com/about/.*

Keuilian, Bedros. "How to Get Things Done Even When Your Business Is in Chaos." Entrepreneur. August 19, 2019. *https://www.entrepreneur.com/article/335271.*

Oprah. "Oprah Winfrey's Official Biography," May 17, 2011. *https://www.oprah.com/pressroom/oprah-winfreys-official-biography/all.*

Robbins, Tony. "About Tony Robbins." Accessed February 24, 2021. *https://www.tonyrobbins.com/biography/.*

Shekshnia, Stanislav, Kirill Kravchenko, and Elin Williams. "The Four Essential Roles of a CEO." Insead: The Business School for the World. March 13, 2018. *https://knowledge.insead.edu/leadership-organisations/the-four-essential-roles-of-a-ceo-8591.*

www.ingramcontent.com/pod-product-compliance
Lightning Source LLC
LaVergne TN
LVHW012041160826
845678LV00014B/2660

* 9 7 8 1 6 3 6 7 6 7 2 6 0 *